THE BURNING
OF WASHINGTON:
August 1814

THE
BURNING OF
WASHINGTON:
August 1814

Mary Kay Phelan

ILLUSTRATED BY JOHN GRETZER

THOMAS Y. CROWELL COMPANY   New York

OTHER BOOKS BY MARY KAY PHELAN

Four Days in Philadelphia—1776
Midnight Alarm: The Story of Paul Revere's Ride
Mr. Lincoln's Inaugural Journey
Probing the Unknown: The Story of Dr. Florence Sabin
The Story of the Boston Tea Party
The Story of the Great Chicago Fire, 1871

Designed by Elliot Epstein
Manufactured in the United States of America

Library of Congress Cataloging in Publication Data
Phelan, Mary Kay.
    The burning of Washington: August 1814

    Bibliography: p.
    SUMMARY: Examines the events preceding, during, and after the British
campaign to capture Washington, D. C., during the War of 1812.
        1. Washington, D. C.—History—Capture by the British, 1814—Juv. lit.
[1. Washington, D. C.—History—Capture by the British, 1814. 2. United
States—History—War of 1812] I. Gretzer, John, ill.
II. Title.
E356.W3P47   975.3'02   74-30025
ISBN 0-690-00486-9
        2   3   4   5   6   7   8   9   10

Especially for
Todd Moore Phelan

ACKNOWLEDGMENTS

Newspapers published in 1814, diaries, letters, notes, and papers of the individuals involved have been invaluable in the writing of this book. Nothing has been fictionized; all conversations are based on the reports of the participants.

To the librarians of the Manuscript Division, the Newspaper Room, and the Rare Books Room in the Library of Congress—special thanks are due. They gave much time and energy to assist me in ferreting out the facts.

The enthusiasm of my husband Martin and our children—Jerry, Dick, and Edna—has been a constant source of inspiration.

FOREWORD

The poet Carl Sandburg often said that "Whenever a people or an institution forgets its early hard beginnings, it is beginning to decay." Fortunately for the young people of today, authors like Mary Kay Phelan are delving into the past, researching and writing history that helps us better understand these "early hard beginnings" of our great nation.

In this well-documented book on how the War of 1812 affected Washington, D.C., Mrs. Phelan traces carefully the movements of both the American and British forces, the woeful lack of preparation in the capital city, the holocaust of the enemy's attack, and the determined recovery of the local citizens. President James Madison and his wife, Dolley; Secretary of State James Monroe; the American commandant, William Henry Winder; the commanders of the British forces, Rear Admiral George Cockburn and General Robert Ross are no longer mere names in a classroom textbook. Under the author's skillful writing, they become real people.

Also woven into the story are a number of lesser known but important persons who played a part in this historic event. There's Dr. William Thornton, designer of our National Capitol, persuading the British not to burn his Patent Bureau; editor Joseph Gales, Jr., of the *Daily National Intelligencer*, lulling the citizenry into complacency concerning the dangers of invasion; French John assisting the First Lady in her efforts to save the valuables from the President's House.

By using present-tense prose, the author has achieved a sense of on-the-spot reporting; thus the reader becomes involved as an active participant. Without hesitation, let me recommend *The Burning of Washington: August 1814* as an exciting and dramatic insight into the tragedies that were a part of our "early hard beginnings."

Fred Schwengel, President, United States
Capitol Historical Society

CONTENTS

One

STARTLING NEWS

It's hot—stifling hot—in Washington City on this morning of August 18, 1814. The residents here are vaguely aware there's a war going on with Great Britain. But no one gives it much thought; the fighting has taken place in such remote spots—on the high seas, in Canada, and around the Great Lakes. The British will never come near this drowsy little town of some nine thousand

citizens, so why worry? Besides, Secretary of War John
Armstrong has repeatedly stated that the enemy could
not possibly want the new nation's capital—"This sheep
walk," he labels it with disdain.

About 10 A.M. people loitering along Pennsylvania
Avenue are startled by the noisy clatter of hoofs. A
dust-covered horseman gallops at top speed down the
broad, unpaved roadway. He reins up in front of the
President's House and runs toward the little building just
to the west, the structure which President Jefferson had
built several years ago "to handle office work away from
the mansion."

Inside the building President James Madison is seated
behind his desk, conferring with Secretary of State James
Monroe. A native of Virginia, Madison is the fourth
Chief Executive of the new country. Just last year he was
elected to a second term of office. Small in stature (he's
only five feet, six inches tall), the sixty-three-year-old
President is anything but impressive in appearance. The
old-fashioned knee breeches and black waistcoat which
he always wears only serve to emphasize the thin pale
face, the watery blue eyes, the wispy gray hair. One of
the day's prominent writers, Washington Irving, un-
kindly described him as "a withered applejohn."

Nevertheless, James Madison has a brilliant mind and
has been in public life ever since his graduation from
Princeton. Often called the "Father of the Constitu-
tion," he has distinguished himself in Congress and more

recently served as Thomas Jefferson's Secretary of State. Too often he fails to impress people with the forcefulness that is expected in a wise administrator. But his weak voice belies the firmness, the integrity of the man himself. To the public he looks reserved, forbidding, even dour. Yet when James Madison can forget the cares of his office for a few hours, he has a certain gentle gaiety, a whimsical manner that endears him to close friends.

Now, answering an insistent rap on the door, Mr. Madison is astonished to see the breathless messenger who has just ridden in from Point Lookout, the observation post seventy miles south of the city. Thomas Swann, the voluntary military observer stationed there, has asked him to bring word that the British have been sighted sailing into Chesapeake Bay. There are more than fifty ships in the fleet; Swann fears this may mean invasion.

Thoroughly alarmed, the President asks the messenger to alert Secretary of War Armstrong over at the War Department building. Although every member in his Cabinet believes there is no danger, an attack on Washington City is what James Madison fears most. He is well aware that Fort Washington, the defense post twelve miles down the Potomac, would not be much of a hinderance. At this very moment it appears that an invasion of the capital is a good probability.

It's been a strange war, an unpopular war—one which few people have understood. Rumblings of discontent began more than ten years ago. England and France had been fighting since 1803. Both countries had refused to recognize the neutrality of American merchant ships. Thomas Jefferson, then President, was afraid that open hostilities with one or the other of these countries might result. He asked Congress to pass the Embargo Act, forbidding all commerce with France and England. (The President hoped this would cause British merchants to lose so much trade that they would demand that the rights of American ships be respected.)

As a result of the drastic embargo, the port cities of New England were devastated. Ship owners and merchants went bankrupt, seamen had no jobs, and the ships began rotting in dry dock. New Englanders were bitterly resentful; some even suggested seceding from the United States and negotiating a separate peace with England.

Soon after Mr. Madison took office, the hated embargo was lifted. Commerce was resumed. Shipping once again became a highly profitable venture. But the people in the port cities had not forgotten what Congress had forced on them.

The war in Europe continued and the powerful British navy ruled the seas. Still, there was the problem of providing enough crewmen for the many ships of His Majesty's fleet. Few men enlisted voluntarily. Living conditions aboard ship were miserable, often unhealthful. Treatment was sometimes brutal. Pay was low and there were times that ships did not come into home port for several years. Many of the crewmen were dragged from debtors' prisons or seized in the street. Whenever possible, these men deserted their ships, often fleeing to the United States.

A strange practice prevailed in the British navy. Each ship's captain was responsible for having a full crew aboard; if he didn't, he lost his command. As the war with France dragged on, the need for men became desperate. The practice of stopping foreign ships on the high seas was more and more common.

Groups of British soldiers, known as "press gangs" would board the ship on the pretext that they were searching for men who had escaped from the Royal Navy. Few of the ships' crews had any papers to prove their nationality; captains, fearful of the consequences, failed to protect their men. Before long, American seamen as well as British deserters were being taken—a procedure known as "impressment of sailors." Such high-handed tactics were infuriating. This was a dramatic infringement of personal liberty and cries for retaliation arose.

Meanwhile, the new nation was expanding westward. There was trouble with the Indians as the settlers opened up more territory. Many believed that the British were inciting the Indians, even paying them to attack and murder the pioneers as well as burn their homes. There was much talk about driving the British from Canada and annexing that country to the United States. Such ideas were put forth in Congress by a fiery young group known as "War Hawks." Led by Henry Clay, these impulsive and energetic debaters cried out for vengeance, for glory, for war . . . war with Great Britain. New England folk, however, wanted no part of hostilities that would again ruin their trade with Europe. The country was divided as never before.

President Madison had tried everything possible to avoid a conflict, but the War Hawks were too strong. On June 18, 1812, a declaration of war was put before Congress. The vote was close, the motion for war being carried in the Senate by only *six* votes. After twenty-nine years of "peace," the new nation was again plunged into battle with Great Britain. Tension ran high, both for and against the war.

Those who were opposed derisively called it "Mr. Madison's War." The governors of Connecticut, Rhode Island, and Massachusetts proclaimed they would send no men to fight. New England bankers refused to loan the government money. The New York *Commercial Advertiser* headlined Congress's declaration as "The Most Awful Calamity."

But on the frontier, the pioneers were wildly enthusiastic. Ranger companies quickly formed; young men drilled constantly and held target practice. They could scarcely wait to get into battle. The fact that America was ill-prepared to fight was no deterrent.

The regular American army consisted of some 7,000 men, who were supposed to defend a nation of almost eight million people. In reality, the country depended upon a militia system—men in each state who were a kind of "home guard," men to be called up in an emergency only, men who were not trained to fight and who had little or no equipment. The British navy, with more than one hundred first-class ships, controlled the seas; against them was pitted the American navy with only sixteen fighting vessels.

During these past two years the American forces have had more defeats than victories off the coast of New England and through parts of Canada. Only on the Great Lakes have there been any real successes. There had been great rejoicing in April, 1813, when troops under command of Brigadier General Zebulon Pike captured the town of York, the capital of Upper Canada, and managed to burn the Parliament building as well as part of the barracks. Of course, people have been deprived of supplies from Europe because of the British blockade along the East Coast. But, for the most part, the war has seemed very far away to the citizens of Washington City. They've become complacent about the whole affair.

Some months ago there was a hint that London might be ready to negotiate. President Madison appointed a five-member Peace Commission, headed by Albert Gallatin. But the British have made no further moves; the peace commissioners are still waiting in the English capital for new developments. Almost daily they are angered by the tirades in the British press. The *London Times* calls Madison "an imposter" . . . "wretched tool" . . . "liar" . . . "serpent." And the *National Register* labels him "an ambitious madman."

Early last April Great Britain succeeded in defeating France, sending Napoleon into exile. As a result, thousands of troops became available for fighting in America. The press continues its attack, urging Parliament to "not only chastise the savages into present peace, but make a lasting impression on their fears."

On May 6 Albert Gallatin had penned a letter to President Madison, describing this new turn of events. He concluded by writing that "there can be no doubt that if the war continues, as great a portion of that disposable force as will be competent to the objects of the British government will be employed in America . . ."

It was late June before Gallatin's letter reached the President's desk. But its contents confirmed Madison's fears. With the addition of many more soldiers, the British would possibly try an attack on the unprotected capital city. There was no time to waste.

Knowing Secretary of War Armstrong's complete indifference to such a possibility, President Madison called on James Monroe to help set up a defense plan. Together they had decided that a new military district—the Tenth—should be created to safeguard the capital. It was to be comprised of militia from "the state of Maryland, the District of Columbia, and that part of Virginia lying between the Potomac and the Rappahannock."

Madison had asked Brigadier General William Henry Winder to command the new Tenth District. The thirty-nine-year-old Winder was a Baltimore lawyer during peacetime and had seen little military service. However, he was a nephew of the Governor of Maryland, and that state, though bitterly divided over the war, must provide a large number of militia for the new district. The President was anxious to win the support of Governor Levin Winder and felt it would be good politics to appoint his nephew as the commanding general, despite the opposition of Secretary of War Armstrong.

On July 1 Madison invited his Cabinet members to the President's House for a conference. After citing the grim possibilities of an attack on Washington City, he outlined his plan for defense. With the Cabinet's approval, the new district was officially created on July 2.

Authorized to summon six thousand Maryland militia, General Winder had suggested to Secretary of War

Armstrong that at least half of that number be called at once and encamp at some point between Baltimore and Washington City. Armstrong scoffed at the idea. He believed that militia needed no training, no drills. They fought best, he said, when called up on the spur of the moment.

Winder lodged a vehement protest. "Should Washington, Baltimore or Annapolis be their object," he wrote, "what possible chance will there be of collecting a force, after the arrival of the enemy, to interpose between them and either of these places?" Further, he added, if the winds were favorable, an expedition could sail up the bay and march to Washington in a day and a half.

Secretary Armstrong failed to answer Winder's letter. Though directed by President Madison to stockpile military stores, he did nothing. Continuing to believe that Washington City would never be the object of an enemy attack, Armstrong refused to strengthen the capital's defenses. By mid-July Canadian newspapers reaching Washington City revealed that thousands of British troops were bound for America. Still Armstrong remained aloof. There was no danger whatsoever, he kept insisting.

Meanwhile, General Winder had become a whirlwind of activity. No detail was too small for his personal attention. He dashed madly about the countryside, looking over the terrain and trying, with little success, to develop some strategy for defense. A report was circulated through the capital that a British admiral had said, "I believe Mr. Madison will have to put on his armour and fight it out." No one had paid much attention.

By mid-August a scorching heat wave settled over the city. Congress had adjourned. Many of the wealthy residents had gone to their country places or were "taking the waters" in Maryland and Virginia. It was really too sultry to worry about what might happen.

But now, on this morning of August 18, President Madison's worst fears seem confirmed. Secretary of State Monroe, too, believes that Washington City may be the object of an enemy attack. During the Revolutionary War Monroe had been a cavalry colonel; when this war began two years ago, he had wanted a field command. President Madison had refused the request, saying that Monroe was needed more in his present position.

However, the thought that the British are nearby prompts the Secretary to ask if he may take some volunteers and ride out to gather intelligence about the enemy's movements. The President agrees this is a good idea and says he will be glad to have a firsthand report. The necessary orders are written and Monroe hurries out, anxious to start on his mission.

It does, indeed, appear that the capital may be in grave danger. Always a meticulous man, President Madison straightens the papers on his desk and hastens over to the mansion to find his "beloved Dolley." Soon everyone will know about the ships sailing up the Chesapeake Bay. He can only hope that fear of enemy intentions will not create chaos in Washington City.

Two

THEY WOULDN'T
DARE!

In the spacious dining room at the west end of the
President's House, a gray-clad figure stands gazing at the
portrait of General George Washington. Dolley Madison
always dresses in colorful satins and velvets for entertaining, but for her morning tasks she still dons the plain
gray gown and white apron of the good Quaker
housewife. Now she inspects the life-size canvas painted

by Gilbert Stuart—one of the prized possessions in the mansion.

When the Madisons had first moved into their new Washington City residence, Architect Benjamin Latrobe helped with the furnishings. Dolley had wanted to place the handsome portrait in the oval drawing room, but Latrobe said, "The dining room is properly the picture room." He had insisted that the portrait must be hung there. Certainly "the father of his country" has been a good influence on the lavish dinner parties which crowd her social schedule.

The brilliance of the First Lady's entertaining is something she has acquired since her marriage to the man she affectionately calls her "darling little husband." Born a Quaker, the first twenty-five years of Dolley's life were spent quietly in Philadelphia, following the strict traditions of her sect.

At twenty-one, she married John Todd, a young lawyer. Three years later he died, and the widow Todd continued to adhere to her Quaker background. However, her radiant personality could not help but attract admirers. Though not beautiful, the dark-haired Dolley was often called "a handsome woman." Tall and erect in her carriage, there is an elusive charm about the soft oval face, the impish smile, the dancing blue eyes.

In 1794, after a whirlwind courtship of four months, Dolley wrote a friend that she had given her hand "to the man who of all others I most admire." That man was

James Madison, the brilliant statesman, already distinguished in the political affairs of the new republic.

During the first few years of their marriage, the Madisons lived in Philadelphia. And it was during this time that the young wife began studying the manners and customs of fashionable society. This was her job, she felt, just as "public business" was James's job. Soon she was donning extravagant gowns, sending to Paris for the latest modes. The towering headdresses of jeweled fabrics—turbans, she called them—became Dolley Madison's trademark.

When Thomas Jefferson was elected President, he appointed James Madison as his Secretary of State. To the dismal social scene in Washington City, Dolley brought exciting new life. There was a continual round of teas, receptions, and dinners in the house at 1333 F Street which the Madisons rented. President Jefferson, a widower, often asked Dolley to be his hostess at executive mansion parties whenever there were ladies present. One visitor recalled that Mrs. Madison was notable for her "good humor and sprightliness, united to the most affable and agreeable manners."

Though the Madisons are mutually devoted, Dolley has never been a political confidante of her husband. "You know I am not much of a politician," she had once confessed to James. "I believe you would not desire your wife to be the active partisan, nor will there be the slightest danger while she is conscious of her want of

talents." Friends and enemies alike have been invited to their parties. Dolley's tact for diplomacy is one of her outstanding characteristics.

Now, on this sultry Thursday morning, the First Lady looks pensively at the portrait of General Washington. How would the nation's first president react to this strange war against an enemy which he, as Commander-in-Chief, had defeated only thirty-one years ago? The sound of footsteps hurrying down the hallway interrupts Dolley's musing. She turns to see her husband entering the room. From the stunned expression on his face, the First Lady knows the President has disturbing news.

Hastily James Madison tells his wife that the British fleet has been sighted sailing into Chesapeake Bay. He knows nothing further, but there is a possibility that Washington City may be their objective. He advises her to begin making plans, just in case they are forced to depart quickly. Now he must hurry back to the office, since he's called a Cabinet meeting to confer on the present emergency.

There have been so many dire warnings this past year—all anonymous, all threatening. Stories of British spies have flooded the capital city; yet no one has proved anything. Dolley recalls a letter she had sent just last month to Mrs. Gallatin, wife of the Peace Commissioner, in London. "They say," she had written, "if Mr. Madison attempts to move from this house in case of attack they will stop him and that he shall fall with it. I am not the least alarmed at these things, but entirely disgusted and determined to stay with him." It's all seemed so improbable . . . something that would never really happen.

Dolley stares around the room in disbelief. Is it possible that this new capital—this "Federal City" built especially for the new republic—may soon be the object of enemy attack? It seems incredible. Why, it was just twenty-four years ago that Congress, then meeting in New York City, had passed "An Act for Establishing the Temporary and Permanent Seat of the Government of the United States."

The lawmakers had decided to move to Philadelphia while the new city was being built, but the Act stated that "on the first Monday in December, 1800, the seat of the government of the United States shall, by virtue of this act, be transferred to a district not exceeding ten miles square, to be located . . . on the river Potomac." To honor the first President, Congress decreed that the city would be called "Washington" and the district, Columbia (after the discoverer of America). With great modesty, however, President Washington always referred to the new home for government as the "Federal City."

The states of Maryland and Virginia agreed to cede land for the district. The President was asked to choose the exact location. After riding up and down the Potomac shoreline for eighty miles, Washington decided on the place where the Anacostia and Potomac rivers meet, a place of great natural beauty just twelve miles above his beloved Mount Vernon.

During the Revolutionary War a young French engineer, Major Pierre Charles L'Enfant, had served under General Washington. When the decision to build the new city was made, the President asked L'Enfant to draw up plans and select sites for the two most important buildings—"the home of Congress" and the "President's House."

After inspecting the terrain on horseback, the versatile young engineer returned to his drawing board. Envisioning something similar to his native Versailles, he drew plans for a capital city that would typify the great nation he was sure America would become, plans that specified broad avenues, graceful circles, and beautiful parks. He chose the highest point, Jenkins Hill, as the site for the Capitol itself and described the location to the President as "a pedestal waiting for a monument." From the Capitol, L'Enfant planned a wide sweeping mall leading to the place where the President's House should be situated beside the Potomac River.

Washington was pleased with the Frenchman's plans and immediately appointed three commissioners—Thomas Johnson, Daniel Carroll, and David Stuart—to oversee the work of building. Two architectural competitions were announced in newspapers throughout the country; one for a design of the Capitol, and another for the President's House. The winner of each was to receive five hundred dollars and a gold medal.

From the many drawings submitted for the President's House, the handsome Georgian-style residence designed by James Hoban was chosen. The Irish-born architect had come to this country several years ago and settled in South Carolina. He was asked to oversee the building of the house, and on October 13, 1792, the cornerstone was laid for this home of Presidents, the first government building to be constructed in the new Federal City.

Meanwhile, drawings were also being submitted for the Capitol. Yet the Commissioners found that none of the plans was suitable. Two months after the contest closed, Dr. William Thornton, a physician who was also an amateur architect, asked if he might send in a belated entry. His design for a stately building with two wings connected by a domed center delighted everyone. "Grandeur, Simplicity and Convenience appear to be so well combined in this plan . . ." President Washington wrote the District Commissioners, "that I have no doubt of its meeting with . . . approbation from you." On September 18, 1793, the cornerstone was laid with appropriate ceremony.

In stipulating ten years for the building of the new government seat, the Congressmen had thought they were allowing plenty of time for completion of the Capitol. But work progressed much more slowly than expected. Because of difficult transportation the building materials were often long overdue. Skilled carpenters, masons, bricklayers, and stone cutters were hard to find. Even unskilled laborers were scarce. There were many financial problems. When Congress had no more money to appropriate, city lots were sold to obtain funds.

Despite endless delays, the government had moved to Washington City during the summer of 1800. Only the North Wing of the Capitol was completed. And in the Senate Chamber on November 22, 1800, President John Adams addressed the first Joint Session of Senators and Representatives. "I congratulate the people of the United States on the assembling of Congress at the permanent seat of government," he said, "and I congratulate you, gentlemen, on the prospect of a residence not to be changed . . . May this Territory be the residence of virtue and happiness . . ."

When President Adams's wife, Abigail, arrived in late November she was shocked at the state in which she found their new home—the great house of white sandstone. Situated in the midst of rough fields, its grounds were cluttered with old brick kilns, stacks of rubbish, and wooden shacks used by the workmen. Inside, only six rooms were finished. There was no plumbing; the thirteen fireplaces were the only source of heat. Because there was no drying yard, Mrs. Adams was forced to hang her laundry in the great unfinished "audience room"—the East Room.

Detailing the many inconveniences in a letter to her daughter, the First Lady concluded by writing: "It is a beautiful spot, capable of every improvement . . ." She somehow managed to hold weekly "drawing rooms" for those who wished to call at the President's House, following a precedent set by her dear friend, Martha Washington, when the executive mansion had been located in Philadelphia.

With the inauguration of Thomas Jefferson in 1801, the Adamses left their residence without regret. Slowly, very slowly, the interior was completed. The yard was leveled; trees and shrubs were planted to relieve the barren landscape. And it was President Jefferson who designed the low-lying wings for either side of the house. Disguised behind colonnades, they provided space for stables, saddle rooms, storage for coal, wood, and wine, an icehouse, a meat house and even a hen house. Architect Benjamin Latrobe was put in charge of construction. He, together with President Jefferson, also drew plans for the North and South porticoes. These, however, are still in the design stage; nothing further has been done about them.

When the Madisons came to live in the President's House five years ago, Congress appropriated six thousand dollars for furnishings. Dolley was ecstatic. Now she could create the elegant setting which she felt was essential to the role of First Lady.

Architect Latrobe was commissioned to assist Dolley

in the decorating. After they had worked out plans for the new furnishings, Latrobe scoured the markets in Baltimore and Philadelphia to find the fabrics, the silver, the china that the First Lady had specified. He also designed a suite of furniture for the Oval Room which Baltimore cabinetmakers John and Hugh Findlay executed with great skill—graceful low sofas matched to delicate high-back chairs. Dolley's fondness for yellow was reflected in the imported damask draperies framing the tall windows of the drawing room. Elaborate mirrors placed at strategic points expanded the great chambers. Handsome art objects decorated the mantlepieces; ornamental lamps added grandeur. But for Dolley the superb touch was the beautiful pianoforte, something she had always longed for.

Young Elbridge Gerry, son of Madison's Vice-President, was a frequent visitor at the President's House. In his diary he recorded his impressions:

The President's House is a perfect palace. You enter the front door and are at once in a large hall, which is as an entry. Pillars of immense size are dispersed thro' this: and it is handsomely furnished, etc., and has large lamps for the whole length. On the side opposite to the entrance are doors opening to four rooms. The corner is the dining room and is very spacious, and twice the height of modern parlours and three times as large. At the head of the room, General Washington is represented as large as life.

This room opens by a single door into Mrs. Madison's

sitting-room which is half as large. This is furnished equally as
well, and has more elegant and delicate furniture. Her portrait
is seen here. This room, in the same way, enters into the
drawing-room, which is an immense and magnificent room, in
an oval form. . . . A door opens at each end, one into the
hall, and the opposite one into the terrace, from whence you
have an elegant view of all the rivers. . . . These three rooms
are all open on levee nights.

As First Lady, Dolley is the undisputed leader of
Washington City society. Her popularity has made the
social life of the administration gracious and brilliant.
Her calendar is filled with an endless round of calls,
receptions, and parties. In addition, she has held
Wednesday evening "drawing rooms." No invitations
are issued; none are needed. To these weekly affairs
come politicians and diplomats, Congressmen and government officials, as well as people of fashion.

"Queen Dolley," as she is sometimes called, is a
charming hostess. No detail for her guests' pleasure is
ever forgotten. At their dinner parties the First Lady
always presides at the head of the table. Her husband
prefers it this way, for it relieves him of the chore of
directing conversation. And Dolley is most adept at
sparkling "small talk." The artist William Dunlap has
described her as "the leader of everything fashionable in
Washington City."

Now that she has received such disturbing news from

her husband, Dolley wonders if it's possible there will be no more parties in this beautiful house. The British couldn't be *that* cruel—or could they? Distracted by worry, the First Lady hurries through the rooms, trying to decide what must be saved if they should be forced to abandon the President's House.

From an upstairs window she catches sight of the Capitol at the far end of Pennsylvania Avenue. It was just seven years ago that the South Wing was finished and the members of the House of Representatives moved in, pleased to have their own chamber. At present a wooden arcade joins the two wings, but Dr. Thornton's design includes a handsome rotunda which should replace the passageway in the near future. Congress has recently established a library, appropriating five thousand dollars to buy reference books for its members. There is still much to be completed in this new seat of government but the Capitol and the President's House are solidly constructed. Certainly these great buildings can withstand any destructive tactics the British may try!

Three

THE CITIZENRY
ALERTED

News of a probable British invasion swept through the
capital like brushfire. By noon a crowd has gathered
around the office of the *Daily National Intelligencer* at
Sixth Street and Pennsylvania Avenue. Though most
citizens are waiting for the latest bulletins, some mutter
angrily about Editor Gales and the way he has played
down any danger to Washington City.

For the past fourteen years the *Intelligencer* has been the most reliable source of news for the town. Early in the summer of 1800 presidential candidate Thomas Jefferson had talked with a promising young journalist, Samuel Harrison Smith. At that time Smith was the owner and editor of the important Philadelphia *Independent Gazetteer.* Mr. Jefferson had persuaded Editor Smith to move his printing office to the new seat of government and issue a paper which would be "the official organ of the new administration." On October 31, 1800, the triweekly began publication as a modest four-page paper. The first and last pages were devoted almost exclusively to advertising; the inside pages carried congressional proceedings, news, and editorials.

Though a brilliant writer, Smith refused to get involved in controversy. Both his foreign and domestic coverage were excellent. But whenever a political issue was raised, the editor would not take sides. One competitor nicknamed the *Intelligencer* "Mr. Silky-Milky Smith's National Smoothing Plane." Nevertheless, the paper achieved the status of authoritative spokesman for the executive branch of the government. So solid is the reporting that newspapers throughout the country today still base their congressional news on what is printed in this paper.

After the Smiths moved to Washington City, both the editor and his wife, Margaret Bayard Smith, became known for lavish hospitality at Sidney, their country estate. Invitations to their parties were much sought after. One could always be sure of meeting interesting people there.

In 1810 Mr. Smith retired. Then in 1813 President Madison appointed him as the first Commissioner of the Revenue in the Treasury Department. The parties at Sidney have continued, now more numerous than ever. One of Mrs. Smith's favorite pastimes is writing letters, especially to her sister Jane, the wife of Chief Justice Andrew Kirkpatrick of New Jersey. In these letters she details everything that is going on in the new capital, social and otherwise.

When Mr. Smith decided on retirement, he sold his paper to one of his reporters, Joseph Gales, Jr. Gales, a British-born journalist, had fled to North Carolina as a political refugee in 1795. Though now a naturalized American citizen, he is still considered by the English to be subject to British law. Seven years ago Editor Smith hired the talented young writer and assigned him to cover proceedings in the Senate. Since the Senate had no official secretary, the reporter's notes provided the only record. Last year the Senators established a "press gallery" by giving Gales a chair on the front rostrum to the left of Vice-President Elbridge Gerry. (It's been whispered about that these two men borrow each other's snuff boxes while the nation's problems are being argued.)

After purchasing the paper, Gales soon discovered

that he needed assistance and persuaded his brother-in-law, William Seaton, to join him. The partners divide their congressional reporting, with Seaton taking down proceedings in the House of Representatives. (Both use the new labor-saving device known as "shorthand.")

Last year the editors decided there was too much news for a triweekly. They would publish every day. Now the masthead reads:

Daily National Intelligencer
WASHINGTON CITY
PUBLISHED BY GALES AND SEATON
DAILY, AT TEN DOLLARS
PER ANNUM;
PAID IN ADVANCE
NO SUBSCRIPTION WILL BE TAKEN FOR LESS THAN
TWELVE MONTHS

Though he is small in stature and homely in appearance, Joseph Gales's journalistic talents and his warmhearted interest in people have earned him a place of respect in the community. As senior editor, he has continued the original owner's policy of steady, conscientious reporting. Ever since the war began, his criticism of the British has been fearless. It's rumored that he will be a target for attack, should the enemy ever reach the capital . . . that next to President Madison, Gales is the American most hated by the British. Despite these rumors, the editor has done his best to quiet the fears of local citizenry that Washington City might be invaded. In an editorial last May he had recalled the victory at Craney Island. On June 22, 1813, the British were attempting to invade Norfolk, Virginia but had to approach the town by way of Craney Island. The Americans with 700 troops and a line of gunboats had successfully driven back the enemy. Confidently, Gales asserted:

We have no idea of his [the enemy's] attempting to reach the vicinity of the Capitol; and if he does, we have no doubt that he will meet such a reception as he had a sample of at Craney Island. The enemy knows better than to thrust himself abreast of, or on this side of Fort Washington.

Now, as the shouts and insults grow louder outside the newspaper office, Editor Gales continues assembling the ads for tomorrow's paper. Richard Parrot & Company is announcing "New Orleans Sugar just received and for sale. 18 barrels, 1st quality."

A plantation owner wants the following inserted:

$50 Reward for negro named Rans—ran away from my farm about the 4th of July. About 5' 10" high. He went off without any known provocation. I will give reward and pay all reasonable charges. Geo. Pannill, Orange County, Virginia

John Carves has a bay mare that is "strayed or stolen." He will pay five dollars reward and "all reasonable charges." Anthony Holmeal advertises that a stray cow came to his plantation. "The owner is requested to come forward and take her away." Roger

Chew Weightman, a bookseller on Pennsylvania Avenue, has a new shipment of the popular *Life of Wellington.*

There are many, many more to be set in type. And there's still the editorial to be written. Gales pays no attention to the noise outside. He has no time for dissenters and he disdains getting involved in useless arguments.

Across town, in their house at 1331 F Street, Dr. and Mrs. William Thornton have just heard the appalling

news. Will the enemy actually try to invade the capital city, the Thorntons wonder. Will civilian homes be destroyed? The couple decides not to chance the possibility of such a disaster. They will pack up their most prized possessions and move to Georgetown with friends until the crisis subsides.

People in Washington City know Dr. Thornton as an amazingly versatile man. Born in the Virgin Islands, he took his medical degree at the University of Aberdeen in Scotland. In 1787 he came to Philadelphia, a site chosen

because of his Quaker heritage. There he married Anna Maria Brodeau and settled down to practice a variety of professions. One was writing. And he published many papers on medicine, astronomy, art, philosophy, and finance.

Talented as an inventor, Thornton worked with John Fitch on the first American steamboat, incorporating many of his own ideas in this new mode of transportation. When he read about the contest for a Capitol design, he borrowed some architectural books, made his drawings, and startled all his friends by winning the award.

In 1794 President Washington asked the amateur architect to be a district commissioner. The Thorntons moved to Washington City soon afterward so he could oversee the building of the "home for Congress" which he had designed.

When President Jefferson appointed James Madison as his Secretary of State, the couple had difficulty in finding a place to live. Dr. Thornton had known the Madisons in Philadelphia and volunteered to help them find a suitable home. The result was that the Secretary of State and his wife rented a recently completed house at 1333 F Street, next door to the Thorntons.

As neighbors, the Madisons and the Thorntons formed a lasting friendship. Though they differed on political issues, the two men enjoyed each other's company, and at one time jointly owned a race horse.

James Madison felt that Dr. Thornton was one man he could always trust.

Their wives were also companionable. They had tea together nearly every day, sometimes went sightseeing in the half-finished city, and borrowed each other's servants for big dinner parties. After James Madison was elected President, the Thorntons were sure they would no longer be close friends. This has not been the case; they are often entertained at the President's House. And Mrs. Thornton records all such events in her diary.

In 1802 President Jefferson appointed Dr. Thornton as the superintendent of the newly established Patent Office. The job is not a demanding one. It leaves plenty of time for the pursuit of other interests. He sketches, writes poetry, and keeps notebooks on an amazing variety of subjects: taxidermy . . . education of the deaf . . . black colonization . . . better treatment for the insane . . . a talking machine . . . artificial ice.

In addition, Thornton has become something of a celebrity as an architect in the new capital. Many have asked him to draw plans for their prospective residences. Probably his most outstanding design has been Colonel John Tayloe's Octagon House at the corner of New York Avenue and Eighteenth Street, just two blocks from the President's House.

The Tayloes named their new residence "Octagon House" because it has eight sides. However, it's not a true octagon in shape since the facade is semicircular in design. Dr. Thornton had specified brick for the outside walls rather than the popular sandstone because brick could be more easily molded into his plan. The three-story house has a completely unique appearance with its circular entry hall, oval staircase, and diagonally placed rooms.

Though Colonel Tayloe has a plantation in Virginia, he had enjoyed "wintering in Washington" ever since his residence was completed in 1800. Octagon House has been the setting of many festivities. But two years ago the Colonel leased his home to the French government. Their Minister, Monsieur Louis Serurier, occupies the handsome mansion at the present time.

This afternoon while the Thorntons continue packing their valuables, Dolley Madison consults with her faithful servant, "French John," at the President's House. Jean Pierre Sioussat was born in the working-class district of Paris shortly before the French Revolution. The Reign of Terror and the rise of Napoleon had been a frightening experience. He turned to study for the priesthood, then decided to join the French navy. When his vessel reached New York harbor, Jean Pierre escaped by swimming ashore, determined to become an American. Making his way to Washington City, he had found employment at the residence of the British Minister, Anthony Merry. Later, President Jefferson appointed him doorkeeper at the Executive Mansion, a position described as "an office of much greater dignity than that of a mere hall porter." French John became well acquainted with the customs and traditions of the house and has served Mrs. Madison as a trusted friend as well as a confidential employe.

Now the First Lady relates to French John the news that the President has received this morning—that a British fleet has been sighted sailing into Chesapeake Bay. She adds that Mr. Madison fears the capital may be invaded. Together they decide what possessions must be packed and saved, if there is an emergency. Dolley still believes that it's highly improbable. Nevertheless, French John assures the First Lady that he will stay with her—no matter what happens.

Over at McKeowin's Hotel on Pennsylvania Avenue, General William Winder is spending a frantic afternoon issuing calls for help. His room here has suddenly become an unofficial headquarters for defense. With the British about to land, the General discovers that most of his army exists only on paper. He doesn't have the one thousand regulars promised him, nor the fifteen thousand militia Secretary of War Armstrong had said would be ready to fight "in case of actual or menaced invasion."

Reviewing the figures, Winder finds there are scarcely more than two thousand men available, and most of these are raw recruits. It's incredible—such a small force ready to defend the capital against an enemy of unknown strength.

Orders are issued immediately. Couriers gallop off

with messages to General Stansbury in Baltimore and General Hungerford in Virginia. "Summon your militia at once," Winder commands. In addition, special appeals go out to the governors of Pennsylvania and Maryland for additional troops.

To add to the confusion, the more excitable residents are beginning to leave town. The road to Montgomery Court House in Maryland is filled with fleeing families, their possessions pushed in wheelbarrows or pulled along in hand-drawn wagons. Washington City at this hour is in a state of turmoil.

Four

DEFENDERS
AND INVADERS

As the first streaks of dawn color the eastern sky on this
Friday morning, August 19, Secretary of State Monroe
and his scouting force gallop out of the city on their
intelligence-gathering mission. Riding through pine for-
ests and across pasture lands, the men spread out to
search the Patuxent and Potomac River regions, intent
on finding the British.

Fifteen miles up the Patuxent River, Commodore Joshua Barney is waiting with his small flotilla of sixteen gunboats manned by four hundred well-trained sailors. The fifty-three-year-old Barney is a swashbuckling seaman who began his career on a pilot boat at the age of twelve. His daring escapades on the high seas have made him famous throughout the country. During the past two years he has executed a series of swift harassing strikes against the enemy as they raided along the coast. Time after time the British have been angered by these unexpected forays.

At 8:30 this morning his lookout informs him that the British have been sighted; the fleet has already entered the Patuxent River. The Commodore scribbles a note to Secretary of the Navy Jones, informing him of this latest development. He adds that there are rumors through the countryside that Admiral Cockburn has been bragging about his plans "to dine in Washington City on Sunday."

When Secretary Jones receives this note, he dispatches new orders to Barney. Take the flotilla as far up the Patuxent River as possible, but if the British approach, blow up the gunboats at once and return with his seamen to the capital to assist in further defense. Barney and his sailors will be far more valuable to General Winder in combat, he adds, than they would be trying to save the small flotilla.

Meanwhile, stories circulate around Washington City that the enemy has already landed . . . with ten thousand troops. Some say it's fifteen thousand. Stage-coach passengers bound for New York City are spreading wild alarms as they travel along the route.

At General Winder's headquarters orders are being issued to set up an encampment at Wood Yard, twelve miles east of Washington City. All militia arriving through the capital are to be sent to this new camp site. Militia coming from the north should rally at Bladensburg, under command of General Tobias Stansbury of Baltimore. Despite all the activity, Winder still has not developed any overall strategy. His plans for defense continue to be hit-and-miss, subject to the whim of the moment.

When bad news arrives from Pennsylvania, the General is frantic. The five thousand men he had counted on from that state will not be coming, he is informed. The old militia law has expired; the new law is not yet in effect. In desperation Winder dispatches an order to Major General John P. Van Ness, who commands the District of Columbia militia. His men are to mobilize at 6 P.M. at the west foot of Capitol Hill.

In private life John P. Van Ness is a prominent banker. Commanding the District militia is only an avocation, but he has taken his job very seriously. All summer he has been calling on Secretary of War Armstrong, trying to set up more defenses for the capital city. When Van Ness receives General Winder's orders, he hurries over to the Secretary's office. Thoroughly

alarmed, he says he is certain the enemy is going to strike a forceful blow.

Secretary Armstrong agrees. "Oh yes," he says, "they would not come with such a fleet without meaning to strike somewhere, but they certainly will not come here. What in the Devil will they do here?"

Van Ness comments that capturing the seat of government of this nation would certainly be worth their efforts.

"No, no!" the Secretary asserts. "Baltimore is the place, sir. That is of so much more consequence."

Infuriated by the Secretary's indifference to the present danger of Washington City, Van Ness hurries over to call on President Madison. Armstrong, he tells the President, is a fool. And furthermore, General Winder has had little military experience; he has no definite plans to combat an invasion. Won't the President dismiss Winder and let him take command of the capital's defense?

The harassed Chief Executive explains that there is too much to be done. This is no time to change command; he will have to deny any such request. Indignantly, Van Ness whips out a piece of paper and writes his resignation, declaring that he now plans to leave town. He refuses to witness the capital's destruction. After Van Ness departs, President Madison sends word to Brigadier General Walter Smith of Georgetown, ordering him to take over the vacated command of the District militia and report to General Winder.

Since early morning the transports of the British fleet have been dropping anchor in the Patuxent River near the little town of Benedict, thirty-eight miles southeast of Washington City. Before leaving England, British Secretary of War and the Colonies Earl Bathurst had decreed that the command for this invasion should, for strategic reasons, be divided between two men.

Leader of the ground troops is Major General Robert Ross. A forty-seven-year-old Irishman and graduate of Dublin's Trinity College, Ross was one of the heroes in Wellington's recent victory over Napoleon. Behind the bright blue eyes and ready smile, there's a calmness, an assurance that his men respect. The General is a strict disciplinarian who thinks nothing of drilling his troops for ten hours a day. Yet he has the admiration of all his soldiers; he is right with them on the front line, no matter what the dangers are.

Before leaving England, Ross had been given some special instructions by Earl Bathurst. "You will not encourage any disposition which may be manifested by the Negroes to rise upon their masters," Bathurst had cautioned. But then he added that if any individual black men want to help the British, they will be welcomed.

Commander of the invading fleet is Rear Admiral George Cockburn. The forty-two-year-old officer had joined the Royal Navy as a youth and had risen rapidly through the ranks, receiving his battle training under Lord Nelson. Though extraordinarily competent in military matters, Cockburn has a noisy, swaggering personality, tossing off his coarse jokes with a devil-may-care attitude. For the past two years he has commanded the blockade in the Chesapeake Bay, raiding and pillaging the port towns with unbelievable cruelty.

Yesterday afternoon, after much discussion, General Ross and Admiral Cockburn had finally agreed on their plan of attack. The troops will disembark at Benedict and march north toward Nottingham along a road which parallels the Patuxent River. Here is where they hope to find Commodore Barney bottled up with his flotilla of gunboats. They intend to mount a dual attack on Barney—marines and foot soldiers acting together.

The flotilla is the primary target. Once Barney's boats are destroyed, they'll decide what to do next. Cockburn thinks the capital would be a great prize. General Ross is hesitant. He has no cavalry troops—and Washington City would be quite some distance from naval support. Besides, Earl Bathurst has told him before leaving England that his land troops should "not engage in any extended operations from the coast."

Yet it's been amazing to the British as they have sailed up the Patuxent River that there's been no opposition whatsoever to their progress. One of the officers last night wrote his wife that the enemy had totally ignored them, "although the cliffs which occasionally arise on either bank offer facilities apparently irresistible to a people so disposed to hatred and so especially hostile to the Navy of England." Where are the Americans? Are they mounting an offensive at some unexpected point? The men can't help but speculate about such a possibility.

When the first redcoats come ashore this morning at

Benedict, General Ross accompanies them in order to inspect the little village. Much to his surprise, he finds it completely deserted. The residents have left their neat white houses in a hurry without attempting to transport any of their possessions. To Admiral Cockburn's disgust,

Ross issues strict orders that there is to be no looting of the vacated homes. Then he posts pickets around the camp. Be on the lookout, he advises, for any Americans who may be lurking in the nearby woods.

Back in Washington City it's now 6 P.M. The District of Columbia militia begins assembling at the foot of Capitol Hill. The new commander, General Smith, is appalled by what he sees. Few of the men have uniforms; some are even barefoot. There is not a single weapon among the men of Captain John J. Stull's company of riflemen. In disgust the commander dismisses the militia, ordering them to report tomorrow morning, fully equipped. Get shoes, he tells them, and find guns. If there are no guns available, then bring butcher knives.

Just as the men are about to disperse, General Winder rides up to inspect the troops. Are these slipshod, bedraggled brigades actually going to defend the capital city? General Smith explains the situation. They will be better equipped by tomorrow, he adds, hopefully.

General Winder calls the militia to attention. Perhaps he can inspire them with an order he has just issued. Pulling a piece of paper from his pocket, he reads: "Let no man allow his private opinions, his prejudices or caprices in favor of this or that particular arm or weapon to be excuses for deserting his post, but seize on those which can be furnished him, or he can command himself, in order to resolutely encounter the enemy, and prove

that the bravery of free men fighting for their families, their liberties, can render every weapon formidable."

Some twenty miles east of Washington City, Secretary of State Monroe and his scouting party have just halted for the night. Their day's expedition has turned up nothing. Around the camp Monroe posts a strong picket line, fearing the enemy may try a surprise attack. Now as the men become silent, sleep is impossible for the Secretary. Mentally he reviews the day's activities. They have combed the countryside. Where can the British be? Are they actually planning an attack on the capital . . . or is this only a wild rumor?

Five

THE TEMPO
STEPS UP

It's been a long night for James Monroe. Anxiety about the capital city has plagued him. Now, as the sun comes up on this Saturday morning, the Secretary rouses his scouting party. There's no time to waste, he admonishes them. They must get under way at once.

Shortly before 10 A.M. the Secretary and his patrol are plodding up a pine-covered hill three miles from

Benedict. When they reach the top, Monroe peers cautiously through the trees. There they are—a cluster of ships anchored in the Patuxent River below. Quickly he directs his men to a safe hiding place back in the woods and proceeds to take up a lookout position behind a towering pine.

A journalist in the party asks if he may join Monroe—he'd like to be able to write a news story about the landing. The Secretary nods approval. Together they scan the scene through spyglasses, watching as hundreds of red-coated soldiers march off the transports. Studying the enemy encampment on the opposite side of the river, the two agree on an estimate—probably some six thousand men. They search for cavalry horses but see none. Is it possible that the enemy troops will attempt an invasion on foot? And where are the pack mules that carry supplies for the army?

At 1 P.M. Monroe writes an intelligence report for President Madison, detailing his observations to this hour. In summary, he adds: "The general idea is that Washington is their object, but of this I can form no opinion at this time."

The newsman is also jotting down his impressions. "I am now with Mr. Monroe," he writes. "We have this morning reconnoitered the enemy in every direction, and collected every information which the neighborhood affords. At 10 A.M. this day we had full view of all their shipping which lay from Benedict to about eight miles below. I counted 23 ships, several brigs and some few small craft.

"The barges and a number of schooners and three large vessels (say frigates) had proceeded up the river toward Nottingham before we got our stand. From the best information I can get I believe the whole force

landed at Benedict is about 6,000. The distress of the neighborhood is inconceivable." In a postscript the writer asks the President to please forward his story to the *New York Post*, once he has read the contents.

One of the scouting party is sent back to Washington City with the messages for President Madison. But

Monroe decides that those who remain should wait quietly in the forest for further developments. Having now observed the British forces, the Secretary feels confident that the capital can be successfully defended. General Winder will probably be able to muster at least seven thousand men. True, there are only one thousand regular troops and the militia are poorly trained. But in numbers alone the Americans will have the advantage. There's also the fact that they are well supplied with artillery pieces—at least twenty-six guns will be available.

Since 9 A.M. in Washington City, the District of Columbia militia have been gathering on the Capitol grounds. The men appear to be somewhat better equipped than they were last night. Most have begged or borrowed rifles, though one man, Joseph McGuane of Georgetown, has reported for duty with two axes and a bullwhip.

The humidity is stifling, yet no one seems to mind. As the men await further orders, they stand around in small groups, conjecturing on what is about to happen. Suddenly there's a burst of fire from Major Peter's artillery company. News has just been received of a great victory in Canada. The British have been soundly trounced in a bloody battle at Fort Erie. Shouts and cheers split the air . . . it's an exciting moment for everyone.

Early this morning Brigadier General Walter Smith,

who commands the District militia, received a message
from Commodore Barney stating that the British had
actually landed at Benedict yesterday and the men were
coming ashore. However, there's been no further word.
Now, in consultation with his officers, the General
decides that the best plan will be to march east and
encamp at Wood Yard. From there they can await the
enemy's next move.

At 2 P.M. the assembled militia, some 1,070 men,
form ranks. Before giving the command to march,
General Smith reads a proclamation just issued by
General Winder. The men are assured that thousands of
volunteers are on the way to "teach our haughty foe that
freemen are never unprepared to expel from their soil
the insolent foot of the invader."

To the spirited music of Captain John Davidson's
Union Light Infantry band, the troops start down
Pennsylvania Avenue and turn left toward the Eastern
Branch of the Potomac River. Crossing the lower of the
two bridges, they head out through the Maryland
countryside toward Wood Yard.

After marching four miles under a blazing sun,
General Smith calls a halt. The men are tiring. They are
not accustomed to walking so far, especially in this heat.
The commander announces they will camp here for the
night. But where are the tents he has ordered? And the
camping equipment? Checking on ammunition, General
Smith discovers that only two hundred flints have been

sent. More than eight hundred of his men cannot fire their rifles. There's utter confusion. The dispirited troops are not looking forward to spending the night in an open field.

Out at Benedict this afternoon the British are preparing to advance. Admiral Cockburn has just completed regrouping his ships. Some will remain anchored where they are. He will take only a small fleet of armed boats upstream, accompanying General Ross and the combat troops as they march northward along a road that parallels the river.

Ross had hoped that saddle horses could be confiscated after they landed, since only three had been brought over on the boats from England. So far none has been found. Officers will be marching on foot beside their men. There will be no cavalry for scouting patrols. Furthermore, there is no way to transport the artillery pieces. Only two three-pounders and two small howitzers are light enough to be pulled by hand. The larger guns will have to be left on board the ships.

There are, of course, the Congreve rockets—plenty of them. Invented by a British artillery officer, Sir William Congreve, the rocket is a metal tube with a projectile on the head which explodes like an artillery shell. General Ross doesn't like the Congreves—they're much too inaccurate. Yet he knows that to be on the receiving end of one of these rockets is a terrifying experience. Despite their ineffectiveness as weapons, the General hopes they will have a demoralizing effect on the Americans.

Shortly before 4 P.M. the men begin forming in columns. When General Ross appears, a spontaneous cheer goes up, a roar that echoes all through the lines. Overwhelmed by this unexpected tribute, the General removes his hat and bows to the troops. After the order is given to march, the long columns move forward briskly with their commander leading the way.

During the next few hours the British troops find that marching along a sandy roadway is a difficult task. Their endurance has been sapped by weeks of idleness on the transports coming over from England. Packs are heavy with three days' provisions and ammunition. There's not a breath of air stirring. Though many of them have served in Spain, the British soldiers have never experienced anything like today's steaming heat. In addition, the red dust kicked up by thousands of tramping feet envelops the troops like a blanket.

Still, General Ross can scarcely believe his good luck so far. After two days in this alien country, there's been no sign of American troops anywhere. Not a single shot has been fired. Where is this enemy they have been sent to defeat? After six miles of marching, the General calls a halt. Their destination is still some distance away, but the men are too tired to go further. Pickets are stationed around the entire encampment; Ross is taking no chances of a surprise attack.

Meanwhile, back in Washington City, the residents who have not yet left town are heartened by Editor Gales's article in today's *Daily National Intelligencer*. It's entitled:

THE ENEMY

The menacing aspect which the enemy has assumed in the adjacent waters has again called our citizens into the field. As soon as the intelligence which we announced yesterday from Point Lookout reached this city, Gen. Winder issued the necessary orders for embodying the several volunteer corps of this district and for parading and holding the remaining companies in readiness.

We do not pretend to be acquainted with the measures which have been for some time maturing for the defense of this district, and which, were we able, it would be improper to make public; yet we have full confidence in the zeal and ability of the officer to whom, for six weeks past, the protection of the district has been entrusted; and doubt not that provision has been made to meet the present crisis . . . The latest authentic news from the enemy's fleet states that a very strong force had entered the Patuxent on Thursday, and indicated an intention to ascend that river.

We shall lose no time in publishing such intelligence of the enemy's movements as may safely be relied on. In the present state of things, however, the various rumors that will be daily circulated should be received with caution.

After being drenched by a midnight thunderstorm, the British are again on the march northward soon after

dawn on this Sunday morning, August 21. At midafternoon there is a brief encounter with the Americans. A
sharp burst of gunfire from the dense woods alerts
General Ross. He and several of his aides dash out to
investigate but the tangled grasses and the hip-high
weeds impede their progress. By the time they reach the
forested area, they catch only a glimpse of American
riflemen scattering through the thick underbrush. Not a
single shot has found its victim.

The British continue on their way to the village of
Nottingham, arriving about 5 P.M. Admiral Cockburn
had been confident that he would find Commodore
Barney and his flotilla anchored there. Instead, the
Americans have pushed further upstream. Just how far,
Cockburn is unable to determine. He's thoroughly
disappointed, having relished the idea of destroying the
swashbuckling Commodore who has harassed him so
often these past few months.

At Wood Yard, eight miles northwest of Nottingham,
General Winder has taken personal charge of the
American encampment. General Smith and his District
of Columbia militia have arrived. Increasing numbers of
militia are reporting every hour. The force now totals
almost four thousand men and Winder has just learned
that three thousand three hundred have been dispatched
from Baltimore to take up positions near Bladensburg.
He's now more optimistic about being able to repel the

invaders. If only he knew for certain how many Englishmen were on the march. Some wild reports have estimated the number as high as eleven thousand. Can this actually be true?

Shortly after dusk Secretary of State Monroe and his scouting party show up at Wood Yard. Fatigued by two days in the saddle, Monroe decides to spend the night at the American encampment. He asks a courier to stand by while he writes a dispatch to President Madison. His party, he reports, left Nottingham just as the enemy was approaching the little village. In fact, he adds, they were very nearly surrounded but managed to escape just in time. After the courier gallops off, Secretary Monroe confers with General Winder. Monroe still believes there are only some six thousand men in the enemy force. At this point Winder is more confused than ever.

As news filters back to Washington City that the British are on the march northward, Mayor James H. Blake becomes more and more alarmed. He knows that the District of Columbia militia marched out into the Maryland countryside yesterday afternoon. Though not a military strategist, he is certain that the enemy's only path toward the capital will be through Bladensburg. Accordingly, he posts an appeal to the citizenry:

All able-bodied Citizens remaining here and all free-men of color, are required to convene tomorrow morning at 6 o'clock precisely, at the Capitol—and from thence to proceed to a site near Bladensburg, to throw up a breastwork or redoubt, deemed important by the Commanding General, for the defense of our city. Those who cannot attend in person, please send substitute.

Shovels, spades, and pick-axes will be furnished on the spot.

Each man must take his provisions for the day with him.

Later this evening Commodore Barney's lookout brings definite word that Admiral Cockburn's fleet is coming up the Patuxent River. Following Secretary of Navy Jones's orders, Barney selects a skeleton crew to blow up the flotilla, once Cockburn is near. Then he lines up four hundred of his marines and they begin marching overland through the night to join General Winder at Wood Yard. Barney has great confidence in his fighting seamen. They've been well trained. Certainly they, together with the military troops, should have no trouble in destroying the British invaders!

Six

ALARM SPREADS

Very early on this sultry Monday morning, August 22, a messenger knocks at the door of the President's House and delivers the dispatch Secretary of State Monroe wrote yesterday afternoon. After some deliberation, the President pens a reply:

If the force of the enemy be not greater than yet appears, and he be without cavalry, it seems extraordinary that he should venture on an enterprise to this distance from his shipping.

65

He may however count on the effect of boldness and celerity on his side, and the want of precaution on ours. He may be bound also to do something, and therefore to risk everything.

By 7 A.M. the British have broken camp and are on the march again, tramping northward. The road leads away from the river and General Ross realizes they are now out of touch with Admiral Cockburn and his supporting armed ships. There's really not much to worry about though. They have caught only a glimpse of a few American soldiers.

Two hours later Ross and his advance troops approach a fork in the road. If they turn left, they'll be heading for Wood Yard and then on to the capital city. If they turn right, the road leads back to the Patuxent River and on north to Upper Marlboro. Which way should they go?

General Ross hesitates for a few moments. Suddenly there's a rustle in the woods to the left, and the General spots some American horsemen lurking behind the trees. He directs the troops to swing left on the road to Wood Yard, but as he does so, the Americans disappear. Ross waits for further action. Is this the encounter they've been expecting? All is silent.

Then the commander reverses his decision, ordering the redcoats to turn back and take the right-hand fork. Soon they'll again have the support of Admiral Cockburn's boats. Furthermore, General Ross is certain that the Admiral's prime objective today is to destroy the American flotilla bottled up in the river. His combat troops will assist in the assault against Commodore Barney and his seamen.

Ross has no way of knowing that at 2 A.M. drums began sounding reveille in the American camp at Wood Yard. General Winder had been unable to sleep, worrying about where the British were hidden. He had decided to seek them out. By sunrise Winder and Secretary of State Monroe were leading an advance party, heading toward the Patuxent River with the support troops following at some distance behind. When Winder and his advance neared the fork in the road, they saw the redcoats turning left.

It looked to Winder as if there were thousands and thousands of enemy troops. Certainly the Americans would be far outnumbered. In panic, Winder gave orders for his forces to fall back. What he did not see was that General Ross had already changed his mind and had taken the right fork in the road, the one leading to Upper Marlboro.

With the Americans turning back, Secretary Monroe scribbles a hurried dispatch to President Madison. "The enemy are advanced six miles on the road to Wood Yard," he writes, "and our troops are retiring. Our troops were on the march to meet them, but in too small a body to engage. General Winder proposes to retire till he can collect them in a full body. The enemy are in full march for Washington City. Have the materials prepared to destroy the bridges."

Meanwhile, the British are heading north again. As they near Pig Point around 11 A.M. a series of violent explosions startle the redcoats. Admiral Cockburn has sighted Commodore Barney's flotilla, but he is too late. The skeleton crew of American sailors left behind by the Commodore are now blowing up the gunboats, as they have been ordered.

Washington City at this moment is in a state of utter confusion. Word has spread that the British are on the march toward the capital. In the building occupied by the State, War, and Navy Departments, State Clerk Stephen Pleasanton is hastily stuffing papers and books into coarse linen bags. These are the government's most important papers—the Declaration of Independence, secret journals of Congress, letters of General Washington, treaties, and diplomatic correspondence. As Pleasanton carries the heavy sacks into the hallway, Secretary of War Armstrong ambles by on the way to his office.

Armstrong chides the State Department clerk for all this frantic activity. It's an unnecessary precaution, he says. And he still does not believe the British are serious in their intention to invade Washington City.

Pleasanton thinks differently. "It's the part of prudence to preserve the valuable papers of the government," he replies, "especially in the face of potential danger." After loading the bulky sacks into a waiting cart, the clerk sets off across the Potomac River bridge leading into the Virginia countryside. He plans to conceal his treasures in Edgar Patterson's empty grist mill. If this does not seem safe enough, he'll go on to Leesburg and place the documents in the hands of the Reverend Mr. Littlejohn, collector of internal revenues for the District.

At the Capitol there are thousands of books and records which must not fall into enemy hands. Clerk of the House Patrick Magruder is vacationing somewhere in Virginia. He can't be reached. But this afternoon his two assistants, Samuel Burch and J. T. Frost, begin searching for wagons in which to haul away the important material. Only one cart drawn by four oxen can be located. The two assistants decide on a hiding place nine miles out of town. This means an eighteen-mile round trip with only one small vehicle. Saving all the records of Congress appears to be a monumental undertaking.

Gunpowder stored across town at the Navy Yard poses a serious problem, too. Clerk Mordecai Booth has been directed to transport the ammunition to a secure hiding place. But how? He's spent most of the day trying to find wagons. Drivers promise to come to the arsenal—then never appear. Others demand exorbitant prices, though one old man insists that Booth take his wagon, saying "Private considerations must give way to the public good." Eventually the clerk lines up five vehicles and loading begins.

Alert to the fears which are enveloping the city,

Editor Joseph Gales is doing his best to calm his fellow citizens. Today's issue of the *Daily National Intelligencer* carries a reassuring message from General Winder:

The enemy threatens the capital of your country, and are now pressing towards it with a force which will require every man to do his duty, without regard to sacrifice and privations. The zeal and promptitude evinced by those now in the field, with the reinforcements which are rapidly pressing to your aid, afford the fairest promise that the enemy will receive the just chastisement of his temerity. Beside those legally called to the honorable and glorious task of defending from insult and

devastation the Capital of your country . . . thousands will voluntarily flock to its standard and teach our haughty foe that freemen are never unprepared to expel from the soil the insolent foot of the invader.

Most of the residents, though, haven't even taken time to read today's paper. They are piling into wagons, carts, hacks—anything with wheels that will transport them to the countryside, and safety. Some are attempting to save cherished possessions but most simply lock their front doors and get out of town as swiftly as possible.

A representative for the New York City firm of Cox & Montaudevert writes his home office: "The distress here is beyond any description. Women and children running in every direction. . . . Expresses are continually coming in from our troops. . . . If the force of the enemy is as large as stated, this city will fall. . . . I have just returned from taking a load of children eight miles out of town, and the whole distance the road was filled with women and children. Indeed I never saw so much distress in my life as today. . . . I am fearful by twelve o'clock tomorrow this city will not be ours."

The French Minister, Louis Serurier, has just finished erecting a pole on the rooftop of his residence, Octagon House. Attached to the pole is the flag of his country. If the British invade the city, Minister Serurier hopes they will realize that this house is under the protection of the French King, that both the house and his family will have "diplomatic immunity."

Earlier this morning it had occurred to Mrs. Joel Barlow, the widow of a prominent Washington City writer, that Octagon House should be a safe place in which to store her most precious art objects. She asked her friend, Mrs. Thornton, to make this request of the Seruriers. The Minister's wife has just written a gracious reply:

Mrs. Serurier has the honor to receive Mrs. Thornton's note. She has given orders to admit into the house Mrs. Barlow's furnishings. In case Mrs. Thornton has anything belonging to her that she would wish to place in her asylum (although she is in hopes that it will be no occasion for it) Mrs. Serurier would be very happy to seize any opportunity she would afford her to be of some service.

As wild rumors continue spreading, there is fear that the slaves may stage a revolt. Someone has already reported that a dangerous conspiracy has been discovered several miles away in the Maryland countryside, that a number of leaders have been arrested. Is such a story true? No one knows for certain. Mayor James Blake is taking no chances. He has clamped a 10 P.M. curfew on the community and asked that all citizens "be vigilant and take up all suspected persons."

At the President's House, James Madison has just received Monroe's dispatch informing him that General Winder has pulled back his troops. Now more anxious than ever, the President seeks out Dolley and asks whether she has the courage to remain here while he goes out to join General Winder and the American troops. He may not be of much help, he adds, but he feels his place is with the fighting forces.

The First Lady does not hesitate an instant. Of course she'll stay here, she says. She has no fear except for him and the success of the American army. The President beseeches her to take care of herself and of "the Cabinet papers, public and private." Reassured by Dolley's confident attitude, Madison asks Secretary of the Navy Jones and Attorney General Richard Rush to join him and his aides in this journey. He also requests his friend, Colonel Charles Carroll, to station a guard of one hundred men around the President's House.

It's nearly midnight when President Madison and his party reach Long Old Fields eight miles east of Washington City. They find that Winder has set up an encampment here. The President decides to spend the night at the Williamses' farmhouse about a mile back of the camp. Attorney General Rush goes to Winder's headquarters tent and reports that President Madison has arrived. The General orders a guard to surround the farmhouse for the night. He will pay his respects to the Chief Executive early tomorrow morning, he promises.

Meanwhile, the British army is already settled at Upper Marlboro. They arrived earlier this afternoon and General Ross had suggested his men rest after such a strenuous march. He detailed a few spies to start searching for the Americans. What is the size of their army? he wants to know. If possible, he would like an estimate of the quality of men under arms.

Tonight the redcoats will bed down in the deserted village. General Ross has been invited to stay at the home of Dr. William Beanes, a physician who is violently opposed to the war with England. Beanes proves to be a friendly host and wants to engage his guest in conversation about the British progress, thus far.

The General, however, has too many problems on his mind to be very talkative. The primary target of this mission was actually to capture Commodore Barney's flotilla of gunboats. Now that the Americans have already destroyed them, should the British turn back down the Patuxent River or continue on to invade Washington City?

Ross knows that Admiral Cockburn is determined to attack the American capital. He's been talking about that for weeks. But is this good military strategy? The troops will be more than thirty miles from the support ships. There is no cavalry . . . actually only four pieces of artillery. Without knowing the number of combat troops the Americans have managed to assemble, the British general is filled with grave doubts. They could be surrounded—and lose everything. Is an invasion worth the chances they'll be taking?

Seven

DIRE WARNINGS

It's still dark on this morning of August 23 when two young British officers saddle their horses and ride out of Upper Marlboro on a mission of their own. These officers, like most of the others on General Ross's staff, are disgusted with their commander and his hesitation in marching on Washington City. With a prize like the enemy's national capital practically within their grasp, how can they turn back now? Knowing Admiral Cockburn's fanatic desire to invade the city, they have decided to seek him out. Perhaps he will have some influence on Ross.

The young Englishmen are not disappointed. The Admiral has spent the night on the tender *Resolution*. Hearing the officers' complaints, however, he dresses quickly and accompanies them back to General Ross's headquarters. The Admiral is very persuasive; finally Ross agrees. Cockburn adds that he will back up the army troops with well-trained sailors from his armed barges. There will be plenty of men, he promises.

Meantime, at 6 A.M. General Winder mounts his horse at Long Old Fields encampment and rides back to the Williamses' farmhouse where President Madison has spent the night. Secretary of War Armstrong has just arrived, too, and wants a briefing on the current situation. Winder knows only that the British are now at Upper Marlboro. According to reports, they have very few horses and just four artillery pieces.

Armstrong still maintains that Washington City is in no danger . . . the enemy would never be foolish enough to try an invasion, especially when they would be thirty miles from any naval support. If by chance they should, the Secretary of War is certain it would be only a hit-and-run attack. He has a pet theory. Why not have Winder hide his combat troops in the Capitol building? When the British were near enough, there could be an all-out strike by the Americans. President Madison thinks this sounds ridiculous and says so. The meeting breaks up with no decisive plans made.

Though there is still much confusion in the capital this morning, Editor Gales has just finished an editorial for today's issue of the *Daily National Intelligencer*. In an effort to discount the hysterical stories that are being repeated, he writes:

THE ENEMY

Nearly all the rumors that reach us from the scene of action are evidently so exaggerated and so contradictory that it is impossible to form from them anything like a correct or satisfactory opinion either of the strength or operations of the enemy. Each man brings the things and fears dictated by his own fears and impressions; consequently we are inundated with numerous reports that bear no likeness to the truth.

In the present circumstances of this District, our readers will find a sufficient apology for the leanness of today's paper. A single object at this time occupies all hands and hearts.

It is 8 A.M. when President Madison, accompanied by Secretary Armstrong and General Winder, rides over to Long Old Fields to review the American troops. The men look dead tired. They've been up since 2 A.M. when by mistake someone had fired a rifle. The General thought it was enemy fire—that the British were on the march. Bugles had sounded and the troops had stood in battle formation until daylight.

As the men march by the reviewing stand in two straggling lines, the President cannot help but wonder about these soldiers. Most of them are in civilian clothes; few have even a semblance of uniforms. However, at the close of the parade comes Commodore Barney who had arrived at Long Old Fields yesterday afternoon. With him are his four hundred seamen, smartly dressed in blue. They are a heartening sight. Perhaps some of their discipline will rub off on the raw militia.

All morning reports continue to come in from scouts who have been observing the British at Upper Marlboro. There's confidence now that the enemy will not leave the village, at least for a while. The President takes time to pencil a note to the First Lady:

The reports as to the enemy have varied every hour. The last and probably truest information is that they are not very strong, and are without cavalry or artillery, and of course they are not in condition to strike at Washington City. It is believed also that they are not about to move from Marlboro, unless it be from an apprehension of our gathering force, and on a retreat to their ships.

Soon after dispatching his message to Dolley, President Madison is informed that two deserters from the British army have just been brought in by one of General Winder's aides, Major Thomas L. McKenney. The President wants to question them. The British provide little information, though they admit that the size of the American army appears to be about the same as the one

they have just left. McKenney adds that he thinks the
enemy will march on them very soon. There's no real
proof . . . it's just his intuition.

Secretary Armstrong discounts any such idea. Even
so, the President feels he must inform his wife.
Hurriedly he writes out a warning to be prepared to
leave quickly and asks a messenger to deliver it to the
First Lady with utmost haste.

Meanwhile, General Winder is devising a plan of
attack, his "victory plan" he calls it. With four thousand
men here at Long Old Fields and the three thousand
Baltimore militia now at Bladensburg, he is confident
that the two forces, if joined together, will find it easy to
encircle the British and drive them out of Upper
Marlboro.

By 2 P.M. President Madison decides there is nothing
further he can do at the American encampment. He and
his party mount their horses and head back toward
Washington City.

Editor Gales in his office at the *Daily National
Intelligencer* has been pleased with reports today about
the citizen-workers who responded to Mayor Blake's
appeal last Sunday. They had turned out in large
numbers, gone to Bladensburg, and erected defensive
earthworks—a patriotic gesture by those who were not
enrolled in the militia. Gales wants to compliment the
black men in particular. And now he writes for
tomorrow's issue that "the free people of color of this

city acted as became patriots: there is scarcely an exception of any failing to be on the spot . . . manifesting by their exertions all the zeal of freemen. At the same time highly to their credit, conducting themselves with the utmost order and propriety."

At the President's House the First Lady has had a distracting day. The one hundred guards, posted around the low stone fence encircling the grounds, have disappeared . . . no one knows where the men have gone. Dolley's faithful servant, French John, wants to spike the cannon at the entrance gate and lay a train of powder which will blow up the enemy, if they try to enter the house. The First Lady vetoes this idea. Her Quaker background rebels at such a proposition. There are some things that can't be done, even in wartime, she explains to French John.

Late this afternoon Dolley tries to take her mind off her worries by writing her sister, Lucy Washington Todd:

My husband left me yesterday morning to join General Winder . . . I have since received two dispatches from him written with a pencil; the last is alarming because he desires I should be ready at a moment's warning to enter my carriage and leave the city; that the enemy seemed stronger than had been reported and that it might happen they would reach the city, with the intention to destroy it.

I am accordingly ready; I have pressed as many Cabinet papers into trunks as to fill one carriage; our private property must be sacrificed, as it is impossible to procure wagons for its transportation. I am determined not to go myself until I see Mr. Madison safe, and he can accompany me, as I hear of much hostility towards him. . . . Disaffection stalks around us . . . .

Dolley's letter writing is interrupted by the appearance of a visitor, George Washington Custis. Custis is the grandson of Martha Washington, the first President's wife. After his parents died, the Washingtons adopted the boy and he grew up at Mt. Vernon. Now he's ridden over from Virginia to ask a favor.

Rumors have spread through the countryside, he explains, that if the British come to Washington City, they plan to invade the President's House. Custis is concerned about the handsome portrait of his grandfather which hangs in the dining room. Will Mrs. Madison be sure that nothing happens to it?

Dolley smiles at the young man, knowing how attached he was to his grandfather. Of course she'll do everything possible to see that no harm comes to the painting, she promises. Reassured, Custis bids Dolley farewell, saying that he hopes that all fears for the invasion are groundless.

It is nearly 5 P.M. when a scout gallops into General Winder's headquarters at the American encampment. He's just seen the entire British army, he reports. They have left Upper Marlboro and are heading toward Long

Old Fields . . . thousands and thousands of men. It looks as if they are preparing to bivouac at the Melwood Estate only three miles away.

Winder is stunned. Now his victory plan is useless. Can the British be plotting a night attack? The American troops, untrained as they are, would be hopelessly lost if the well-disciplined redcoats strike after dark. If he takes his men to join the militia at Bladensburg, the road to the capital would be left wide open. Of course there's the upper bridge to cross before reaching the capital, the bridge across the Potomac River. That must be destroyed at once.

Confused and upset by this unexpected turn of events, the General decides there is only one thing to do—pull back his entire force to Washington City. Soon after sundown the weary troops form up. What starts as an orderly march soon becomes what one artilleryman describes as "a run of eight miles." Three hours later the men swarm across the bridge. Winder sets up camp near the Navy Yard where his disheartened militia will spend the night under the stars.

President Madison has already reached home. He's barely had time to greet his beloved Dolley before visitors start calling on him. Each one has a different idea about what must be done to save the city. One man suggests he can blow up the Capitol himself, to save its destruction by the British. The President refuses permission for any such violence.

Once the encampment near the Navy Yard is established, General Winder hurries over to call on Captain Thomas Tingey who commands the Navy Yard. Will the navy make certain that the upper bridge leading into the city from Long Old Fields will be blown up? Tingey assures him that all preparations have been made. The bone-weary Winder, after informing the President of current plans, returns to his camp.

Shortly before midnight one of Winder's militiamen writes a friend in Philadelphia: "I cannot find language to express the situation of the women and children, who are running the streets in a state bordering on distraction. Some are trying to remove their bedding, clothes, and furniture, while others are determined to stay by their homes until they are burnt around them." The soldier cannot help but wonder what tomorrow will bring.

Eight

DISASTER AT
BLADENSBURG

After less than three hours' sleep, General Winder is up at dawn this Wednesday morning, August 24. The reddish tinge in the eastern sky assures him that in response to orders the upper bridge across the Potomac River has been blown up. Riding over to the Griffith Coombs's house near the lower bridge, the General establishes headquarters here. Various scouts bring in conflicting reports about the enemy's location. Alarmed by the lack of intelligence, Winder pencils a note to Secretary of War Armstrong. "I should be glad," he writes, "of the assistance of counsel from yourself and the government."

The message is mistakenly delivered to the President's House. Madison, after reading it, sends messages to the members of his Cabinet. Assemble at Winder's headquarters as soon as possible, he requests. Within half an hour the President himself arrives at the Coombs house, followed by Secretary of State Monroe and Secretary of Navy Jones. Attorney General Rush joins the conference a few minutes later.

By now there's a hubbub of confusion as more reports filter in. One suggestion after another is offered to Winder but the distraught General makes no decisions. Then someone brings a rumor that the British are heading for Washington City and will enter across the lower bridge. Word is dispatched to Commodore Barney that he and his four hundred sailors are to make a stand at the bridge . . . defend it with their lives, if necessary.

Soon afterward another messenger bursts into the conference. It's Bladensburg. The British, he declares, are definitely marching toward the village. He's seen them himself. This is authentic, Winder decides, and issues immediate orders for his troops to move out and join General Stansbury's Baltimore militia already encamped near Bladensburg. By 11 A.M. the men begin the five-mile march.

The conference breaks up just as Secretary of War Armstrong strolls into the headquarters. The President informs Armstrong that he expects the Secretary to go to Bladensburg at once and give any assistance he can to General Winder. Madison and his Cabinet decide they'll also ride up to the battlefield. First, though, they stop to inspect Commodore Barney's defense of the lower bridge.

When the Presidential party reaches the bridge, they are met by an infuriated Commodore. Why has he been left to guard a bridge when the action is miles away? He wants to take his seamen and head for Bladensburg. President Madison agrees. Go ahead, he instructs, but leave a small detail to blow up the bridge, should the enemy appear.

By noon the British have already arrived at Bladensburg and are taking battle positions. Nestled among rolling hills, the village is situated on the east bank of the Potomac River. Just west of the town a bridge spans the river; two roads branch off from the bridge, one leading to Georgetown, the other to Washington City. On a ridge overlooking the Georgetown road General Stansbury and his Baltimore militia have set up their camp. When a scout reports he has just sighted a steady column of redcoats pouring into Bladensburg, the commanding General is disconcerted. Stansbury is sure the British will overpower them—and soon. But the arrival of the first troops from Washington City is more reassuring.

There has been no plan, no organization for the battle that is shaping up. General Winder has still not worked out his strategy. Individual officers position their troops as they think best, while Winder rushes aimlessly from one group to another.

At 1 P.M. General Ross and his British soldiers begin streaming across the bridge. American artillerymen open fire but the redcoats keep coming. Once on the west bank, the British scatter into the woods and begin shooting. Suddenly, from behind a warehouse in Bladensburg comes a great burst of flame, a shooting projectile of fire aimed at General Stansbury's troops. The first Congreve rocket has been set off, followed by another—and still another. The sight is terrifying; the militia panic and retreat.

Winder attempts to rally his forces, realizing that he must counterattack quickly. He barks out orders; advance, advance! For the next few minutes the Americans seem to be in command. Their cannon, aimed at the oncoming redcoats, is taking its toll.

General Ross changes his strategy. He orders his men to move around behind the Americans, thus cutting off Stansbury's troops from those of Winder. The Congreve rockets continue their devastating effects. Stansbury's units again break up, this time fleeing down the Georgetown road in a disorderly rout. Within thirty minutes General Winder believes the battle is hopeless. Word is passed through the lines to turn back to Washington City.

When the fighting began, President Madison and his party had wisely moved behind the lines. They could still observe what was happening but stayed out of the range of fire. After ordering the retreat, General Winder sends a hastily scribbled warning to the President. Dejectedly Mr. Madison and his party head down the turnpike leading back to Washington City.

Meanwhile, Commodore Barney and his four hundred seamen have just arrived on the scene. Quickly sizing up what has happened, Barney orders his men to take up positions beside the main road. The redcoats move forward in orderly columns. Barney waits until they are almost upon him . . . then orders one battery of guns to begin firing. Several direct hits are scored. For a few moments the road is clear. Then the well-disciplined British regroup and charge forward.

Now Barney shouts to both artillerymen and riflemen:

"Fire, fire, as fast as possible!" Their aim is deadly. Again and again the Englishmen are beaten back by the rain of musket and cannonballs. General Ross recognizes the futility of continuing charge after charge; he orders his men to move around the American sailors, attacking from the side and rear.

The Commodore, once he realizes what has happened, yells to his sailors to assault the enemy with fixed bayonets. Board 'em! Board 'em! is the noisy battle cry. It's a heroic gesture but the thousands of British soldiers are too much for the few hundred seamen.

Barney, badly wounded in the hip, fights on until his strength gives out. Collapsing, he sinks down behind one of the big navy guns with which his men have been pounding the enemy. He asks a sailor standing nearby whether any of Winder's troops can be seen returning to the battlefield. The answer is no.

Realizing that further fighting will achieve nothing, the Commodore now orders his men to withdraw. Three of the sailors want to improvise a litter and carry him to safety. Barney is adamant. He will stay where he has fallen. Everyone else must get out—quickly, quickly.

When a British scout finds the wounded Commodore alone, he calls Admiral Cockburn and General Ross. Ross congratulates Barney on the gallant stand he and his men have made. Since setting foot on American soil, Ross adds, the sailors have given the British their only real opposition. Barney offers to surrender and be taken prisoner. Instead, General Ross paroles him, ordering that the Commodore be carried to a tavern in Bladensburg and treated for his wound.

Before leaving the President's House this morning, Mr. Madison asked Dolley to please have dinner ready about 3 P.M. He intended to bring some of his Cabinet members and a few "military gentlemen" home with him for a small victory celebration. At midmorning the First Lady instructed Paul Jennings, the black serving boy, to set the dining room table. Use the gold-edged china made by Dagoty of Paris and the best silverware. Then bring up the ale, cider, and wines and place the bottles in coolers. Nothing is too good for her husband's guests, Dolley added. In the kitchen, roasts are already turning on spits before the open fire. Pots of vegetables, potatoes, and sauces cook on the fireplace grate.

When news filters back from Bladensburg that a battle is shaping up, the First Lady becomes apprehensive. Where is her husband? Is he safe? Roaming restlessly through the upstairs rooms, she peers out the windows, turning her spyglass in every direction, trying to fathom what is happening. Twice during the morning Mayor Blake called at the President's House, urging Dolley to flee. She remained determined. No, indeed, she asserted, she will not leave until she knows Mr. Madison is safe.

As the day wears on, the distant boom of guns rattles

the windows. To quiet her nerves, Dolley sits down at her desk to continue the letter to Lucy which she started yesterday:

Will you believe it, my sister? We have had a battle or a skirmish near Bladensburg, and I am still here within sound of the cannon! Mr. Madison comes not; may God protect him! Two messengers covered with dust come to bid me fly; but I wait for him. At this late hour a wagon has been procured. I have had it filled with the plate and the most valuable portable articles belonging to the house; whether it will reach its destination, the Bank of Maryland, or fall into the hands of British soldiers, events must determine. . . . When I shall again write to you, or where I shall be tomorrow, I cannot tell!

Dolley is still at her desk when Sukey, her personal maid, rushes into the room. She's just seen Jim Smith galloping up Pennsylvania Avenue toward the President's House. Smith, Madison's freedman, had accompanied the President from the Navy Yard to Bladensburg. Dolley hurries to the window and hears Smith shouting, "Clear out! clear out! General Winder has ordered a retreat." He brings the First Lady a scrawled note from her husband telling her that the battle has been lost. She must leave at once.

Losing none of her composure, Dolley directs her coachman, Jo Bolin, to bring her carriage around to the door. Accompanied by the faithful French John, she hastens into the dining room and snatches up what silver

and china she can stuff into her old-fashioned reticule.
Aghast, the First Lady realizes she has done nothing
about the portrait of George Washington, still in place
on the dining room wall.

The painting is too precious to leave behind, Dolley
tells French John. Get a ladder and take it down at once,
she directs. French John, teetering on the top step,
twists and tugs at the frame, but it will not budge. It is
screwed to the wall, he tells his mistress. Then get the
gardener, Magraw, Dolley orders, and ask him to bring a
screwdriver and an axe. The picture will have to be
chopped away from the frame.

While French John and Magraw work frantically,
Colonel Charles Carroll strides into the room, accompanied by two New Yorkers, Jacob Barker and R. G. L.
dePeyster. Colonel Carroll tells Dolley he has seen the
President, and Mr. Madison sends word that his wife
must leave at once—this very minute.

No, says the First Lady. She cannot do that—not
until she is certain the portrait is safe. Minutes pass.
Colonel Carroll continues to fume at Dolley. Leave the
blasted old picture. If she doesn't hurry, she'll be trapped
by the British. The First Lady remains calm. Finally, the
frame is broken. The canvas, still on its stretcher, is
lifted out. Painstakingly, the portrait is laid on the dining
room floor.

Turning to Barker and dePeyster, Dolley pleads with
them to take charge. Please load the canvas into their

wagon and take it to a farmhouse in the country for safekeeping. There's no other way, she adds.

With the New Yorkers' promise to take care of the precious portrait, Dolley now feels free to leave. She hurries out to the waiting carriage with Sukey at her heels. Coachman Jo Bolin cracks his whip. The horses turn onto Pennsylvania Avenue and head westward toward Georgetown.

It is less than half an hour later when the despondent President arrives home with several of his aides. The men go inside to talk over the disaster which they have just witnessed. Madison says that if he had not been present, he could never have believed that so great a difference existed between well-trained troops and the raw militiamen.

Out on the streets there is bedlam. Knowing their city is now lost, citizens rush toward the outskirts of town. All discipline for the soldiers has vanished. Streaming into town, many hurry to their homes, trying to rescue their families and whatever possessions they can carry.

Secretary of Navy Jones stops at the Navy Yard on his return from Bladensburg. He orders Captain Thomas Tingey to continue removing all ammunitions and stores. But, he adds, if the enemy approaches, the Yard is to be fired at once. Tingey has been commandant here ever since the Yard was founded in 1800. Because of his ceaseless efforts, it is the finest in the country. He knows it will be a bitter hour, indeed, if he has to destroy the work of fourteen years.

Soon after sundown President Madison and his party ride out across the meadow behind the mansion and board a boat which will take them to the Virginia shore. Watching from an upstairs window of Octagon House, French Minister Serurier sees the Presidential party heading for the Potomac River. Sympathy for Mr. Madison is uppermost in his mind as he writes a friend in Paris:

It was then that the President, who in the midst of all this disorder, had displayed, to stop it, a firmness and constancy worthy of better success, but powerless in regard to militia which more than once, in the War of the Revolution, had drawn after it in flight the illustrious Washington himself, coolly mounted his horse, accompanied by some friends and slowly gained the bridge that separates Washington City from Virginia.

The faithful French John remains at the President's House for the next hour, doing the last-minute tasks which his mistress had assigned him. Gently he picks up Dolley's pet macaw and hastens over to Octagon House with the bird, leaving it in care of Minister Serurier's chef. Returning to the mansion, he takes a final look around. After closing all the windows, he locks the front door and deposits the key at the home of the Russian Minister Daschakoff. Come what may, French John is confident he has done everything possible.

Over at 1331 F Street, Dr. and Mrs. William Thornton are among the last residents to leave the city. They've been packed for two days but to flee seemed as if they were deserting their friends, the Madisons. However, soon after sundown, they set out for Georgetown to stay with Dr. and Mrs. Thomas Peter. Tonight Mrs. Thornton records the day's events in her diary:

Wednesday, 24th: No accounts at ten this morning of the course of the Enemy. Almost all our acquaintances gone out of town. Nearly ALL the moveable property taken away— offices shut up & business at a stand.

We heard rumors that the armies had engaged, & expected to hear the cannon etc. but heard nothing—at last saw a man riding as hard as possible toward the President's House—we went up soon after & found that Mrs. M. was gone—We sat down to dinner but I cou'd eat nothing and we dilly dally'd till we saw our retreating army come up the avenue—we then hastened away, and were escorted out of town by our Defeated troops . . .

Nine

THE CAPITOL
IN FLAMES

With the Americans in full retreat, General Ross decides
to rest his troops for a few hours. The furor of battle was
bad enough. But the humidity, the heat of a boiling
August sun have left the men exhausted. Never before
have the Englishmen experienced anything like this.
While the General sets up camp for the larger portion of
his army on the Bladensburg field, Admiral Cockburn
writes a report to London on the outcome of today's

battle. The British could not pursue the fleeing Americans, he explains, because "the victors were too weary and the vanquished too swift."

Soon after sundown General Ross forms a fifteen-hundred-man brigade, selecting those troops who have seen the least action during the afternoon. He wants soldiers who are refreshed for this final assault on the capital. At the sound of bugles, the men line up in columns and begin the march along the turnpike leading directly into Washington City. By 8 P.M. they reach the outskirts of town and halt just inside the turnpike gate.

The two British commanders have already decided to try to extract a large sum of money from the American government in return for not firing on their capital. As conquerors, this will be the prize money to which they are justly entitled. At this moment Ross orders a large white flag hoisted—the truce symbol. Drums roll loud and long, shattering the silence of the night. It's the military signal for a conference with the enemy. They wait for the Americans to come forward. No one appears. The streets are deserted, the houses dark and shuttered.

Moving on with his advance force of two hundred, General Ross leads the men down Maryland Avenue where at the end looms the massive Capitol building— pride of the new nation, a stark symbol of American independence. It's much larger, far more impressive than Ross had expected.

The redcoats approach the corner of Second Street Northeast. On the northwest side is Robert Sewall's handsome home. It had been rented to Albert Gallatin during his long term of service as Secretary of the Treasury. Ever since President Madison sent Gallatin to London last spring as head of the Peace Commission, the house has been unoccupied. From an upstairs window of Gallatin's former residence, a volley of musket fire comes crashing through the darkness. One soldier is killed; three are wounded. And General Ross's horse is shot out from under him.

Surround the house at once, the General commands, shouting for the tenants to come out. All is silent. Ross sends a search party inside with orders to shoot on sight. The house appears to be vacant. It is burned to the ground.

Meanwhile, Mordecai Booth, chief clerk of the Navy Yard, has been sent out by Captain Tingey to scout for the oncoming enemy. When Booth sights the redcoats halted at the turnpike gate, he gallops back to the Yard to inform the Captain. Tingey glances at his watch. It's precisely 8:20 P.M. when he gives the order to set the fires.

All day delegations of nearby residents have been pleading with Captain Tingey not to destroy the Navy Yard. They fear for their own homes. The Captain

explains that orders are orders. If the British invade the capital, he must do what Secretary of Navy Jones has commanded. Nevertheless, the inflammable materials have been placed in such a way that the blazes will not be carried into neighboring properties. Now, seamen scurry about applying matches; in a few moments great sheets of flame light up the sky. Earthshaking explosions rock the countryside.

The rigging loft, the saw mill, machine shops, the timber shed, the paint shops—all are engulfed by the spreading fires. The new frigate *Columbia* was to have been launched in ten days. The sloop *Argus*, just completed, has all her armament and equipment aboard. Only provisions and powder are lacking. Both vessels are swept up in the conflagration along with two old frigates, *Boston* and *General Greene*. Grimly satisfied that he has obeyed orders, Captain Tingey climbs into his boat and rows across to the Virginia shore.

Over at Octagon House French Minister Serurier has been watching the destruction of the Navy Yard from his front windows. He writes the French statesman Talleyrand in Paris, describing the scene:

I have never beheld a spectacle more terrible and at the same time more magnificent. Your Excellency, who knows the picturesqueness and grandeur of the locality, can form an idea of it. A profound darkness reigned in the part of the city which I live in, and one was delivered up to conjectures and to false reports . . . as to what was occurring in the quarter lighted by this frightful blaze.

General Ross now orders the troops still at the turnpike gate to move forward into an open field just east of the Capitol. High weeds and tangled underbrush impede the marching men but it is not long before they are assembled in groups. Here Ross waits for half an hour, still hoping that some authority from the American government will come forward to discuss a settlement with him.

Admiral Cockburn is furious with the General's seeming hesitation. Blow up the Capitol at once, he urges, reminding Ross how the Yankees last year had set fire to the Parliament building at York, the capital of Upper Canada. At that time there had been much British sentiment for retaliation. Very well, agrees Ross. Perhaps there *is* a score to settle.

The troops are lined up, facing the east side of the Capitol. "Fire!" shouts the commander. A volley of bullets breaks the windows of both the House of Representatives and the Senate wings. General Ross details his deputy quartermaster, Lieutenant deLacy Evans, to charge forward with a few men and shoot off the door locks.

Once the way is clear, the redcoats swarm through the building, gazing in awe at the spacious chambers of the American lawmakers. They admire the handsome marble columns in the House of Representatives, columns designed by Benjamin Latrobe with motifs of tobacco leaves and corncobs bordering the tops.

Some help themselves to small souvenirs—leather-bound books, quill pens, snuff boxes. In a room next to the Senate chamber two soldiers are attracted by the portraits of King Louis XVI and Marie Antoinette. They had been presented to the American government by the French king who had aided in the fight for Yankee independence. Recognizing their value, the redcoats cut the paintings from their frames and hide the rolled-up canvases under their coats.

General Ross and Admiral Cockburn are still outside, discussing how they should destroy the Capitol. Gunpowder would be best, they agree, and they've captured great quantities of it on the Bladensburg battlefield. While they stand talking quietly, a group of residents approaches the Englishmen.

Anxiously, the people point out that any explosion strong enough to demolish the massive building will also wreck all the dwellings in the vicinity. The General agrees this is probably true. Further, he assures them, he has no intention of destroying private property unless a cache of firearms is discovered or there is resistance from homeowners. Very well. Rather than blow it up, he will burn the Capitol.

Ross summons naval Lieutenant George Pratt, an expert in demolition. Fire the wooden passageway between the two wings first, he orders. Then proceed to both the House of Representatives and the Senate chambers. Pratt now details three-man teams to each room on the lower floors of the two wings. The first man is to chop up the woodwork for kindling; the second man will sprinkle rocket powder over the floor; the third will follow behind, lighting the powder with a torch.

In the House of Representatives' chamber, Lieutenant Pratt instructs his soldiers to fire rockets through the roof. There is only a dull thud—nothing more. Several of the redcoats scramble up on the roof and discover that it is sheet iron. Other measures will have to be tried.

Pratt notes that the gallery is filled with seats of tinder-dry yellow pine. Mahogany desks, tables, and chairs are thrown carelessly into a large heap on the main floor. Powder is sprinkled liberally over the mound of furnishings and rockets are fired directly at it. The hands of the massive clock above the Speaker's chair point to 10 P.M.

Similar tactics are being followed in the Senate wing of the Capitol. Here, added to the pile of furniture, are the seven hundred and forty books brought down from an upper floor. These are the volumes purchased in 1802 as a beginning for the Library of Congress. With gleeful abandon the soldiers toss the books on the pyramid of furnishings.

Within fifteen minutes both wings are aflame. Great sheets of fire erupt through the broken windows, licking at the outer limestone walls, soaring upward to the roof. More than a building and its furnishings are being consumed at a rapid rate. Papers on claims and pensions, records of the Revolutionary veterans, priceless secret documents . . . all are destroyed.

Admiral Cockburn watches the spectacular blaze at some distance from the building. Suddenly, he spots a crumpled newspaper lying on the ground. It's today's issue of the *Daily National Intelligencer*. The brilliance of

the leaping flames makes it easy to read Joseph Gales's editorial:

Nearly the whole of yesterday passed off without any information of importance from our troops or those of the enemy, except a report, for some time believed to be true, that the enemy had retrograded toward Nottingham. . . . We feel

assured that the number and bravery of our men will afford complete protection to the city. . . . Reinforcements every moment expected will preserve the safety of the city.

Tossing away the newspaper, Admiral Cockburn smirks with satisfaction. Definitely, the savages are getting exactly what they deserve!

In less than an hour the Capitol is gutted, the wooden passageway completely destroyed. Fire in both wings has burned so fiercely that most of the marble columns are reduced to lime. Glass chimneys around the candles have melted into heaping masses. Stairways are blackened and split.

Gigantic flames shooting skyward have illuminated the countryside for more than thirty miles. One British officer describes the sight as "striking and sublime." The few citizens still in Washington City watch from behind shuttered windows, horrified at the destruction the British have inflicted.

Out along the Virginia shoreline the Presidential party is riding through the darkness. Occasionally James Madison looks back, glimpsing the brilliantly lighted sky. All his hopes, his dreams for this new nation are going up in flames!

Ten

FIRING THE
PRESIDENT'S HOUSE

Now that the Capitol is ablaze, General Ross and
Admiral Cockburn start down Pennsylvania Avenue
with a group of one hundred and fifty specially selected
soldiers. Ross on a fresh horse rides at the head of the
first detachment, his men following two-by-two. Their
hands and faces are powder-blackened, their stiff red
uniforms wilted from the heat.

No triumphant beat of drums breaks the ominous silence. Even the tramp-tramp-tramp of marching feet is muffled by the sandy roadway. Ross keeps turning his head from side to side, listening for any suspicious noises. Could General Winder be secretly recruiting his militiamen to catch the redcoats off guard? Are there snipers hidden along the Avenue, waiting to fire?

Following three blocks behind is the second detachment of soldiers, led by Admiral Cockburn. He's seated jauntily on an old mule—the only available mount he could find. The Admiral grins. It's been a great night thus far, with more destruction to come.

At McKeowin's Hotel on lower Pennsylvania Avenue Ross notes a small gathering of residents. He halts the troops as one of the group approaches him. Will the British burn everything, even private homes? the man inquires. There is nothing to worry about, he's told, so long as the citizens stay inside their houses. Why, they're as safe as if the American troops were occupying the city. At this moment Cockburn rides up. In swaggering fashion he reassures the residents that civilized Englishmen, not barbarians, are in control. There's no cause for alarm.

The troops continue their march until they reach the corner of Pennsylvania Avenue and Fifteenth Street Northwest. Here the avenue bends slightly alongside the red brick Treasury Building. Someone spots a town pump in the yard. General Ross suggests the men may want a drink after the two-mile march down the dusty roadway. Up to now, Ross has refused to allow his men to drink any water in the city, fearful that the Americans may have poisoned it. But this seems a safe spot for relieving parched throats.

While the thirsty soldiers line up, General Ross and Admiral Cockburn stomp into Mrs. Barbara Suter's boarding house, just south of the Treasury. Have supper prepared in about an hour, Ross orders. His officers will be hungry after their visit to the President's House; they deserve some of Mrs. Suter's fine food.

The landlady says that McLeod's Tavern a few doors away would be more suitable. It's too late and she has only one serving woman. General Ross is insistent . . . he and his staff members have heard what an excellent cook Mrs. Suter is and they want to sample her fried chicken. Though she has no heart to serve the redcoats, the harassed landlady finally agrees—more from fear of reprisal than anything else.

Once this is settled, General Ross crosses the roadway and leads the troops alongside the low stone fence surrounding the President's House. They turn into the wide entranceway, passing by the imposing gateposts, topped with their bronze eagles. After battering down the front door, the men scatter in all directions, anxious to see where the Chief Executive lives.

Shouts of pleasure ring out as several soldiers discover the dining room table set for forty people. On the

sideboard are handsome glass decanters, each filled with a different kind of wine. Plate holders by the fireplace are stacked with dishes . . . silverware is still on the table. Raiding the kitchen, the men find joints of lamb, roasts of beef, succulent Virginia ham turning on the spits—all somewhat overdone but tasty, nonetheless. Pots of vegetables and potatoes are on the open grates. The pantry is loaded with pastries. For the hungry redcoats this is an unexpected feast; they waste no time in consuming the food.

A few minutes ago Admiral Cockburn, swaggering across the roadway, collared a young American who admits that he is Roger Chew Weightman, a bookseller in Washington City. Cockburn commands Weightman to be his guide through the President's House. Now in the dining room the Admiral pours out generous goblets of wine and insists that Weightman join him in a toast to the President. "To little Jemmy," Cockburn roars, tipping up his goblet and slapping the embarrassed bookseller on the back.

In an expansive mood, the Admiral commands his young victim to pick out a souvenir. Weightman, hoping to retrieve something valuable for the Madisons, starts toward a silver urn on the sideboard. "No, no," says Cockburn, "nothing like that." The valuable pieces, he explains, must be destroyed and he hands Weightman a small candleholder from the mantlepiece. Wandering through the upstairs rooms, the blustering Admiral picks up an old hat belonging to the President, a cushion from Mrs. Madison's dressing table chair, and a roll of letters which he finds stuffed in her desk drawer. The letters, he adds, will make good reading during those lonely nights at sea.

Following the example of the Admiral, other redcoats are seizing souvenirs from the President's House. One soldier is fascinated by Madison's portable medicine chest, a handsome mahogany cabinet with tiny drawers for various kinds of pills. Another redcoat helps himself to a ceremonial sword. Captain Harry Smith discovers that the President's wardrobe is still intact in a bedroom closet. He exchanges his grimy shirt for one of Mr. Madison's finest linen garments. Dolley's turbans, her rhinestone buckles, necklaces—all are stuffed into soldiers' pockets as remembrances of this late-night expedition.

General Ross is in the Oval Drawing Room to oversee destruction of the furnishings. The beautiful yellow damask draperies are snatched from the windows; the specially designed sofas and chairs are piled helter-skelter in the middle of the room. Dolley's pride—the handsome pianoforte—is knocked over; oil lamps and art objects are tossed carelessly on the growing heap in the center of the room.

About 11 P.M. a messenger appears and asks to speak with General Ross. He's been sent by Monsieur Serurier, the man explains. The French Minister has been watching from nearby Octagon House and has become alarmed that the British may attempt to destroy his residence after they have finished at the President's House. Ross pauses long enough to pen a reassuring reply to the Minister. "The French King's house," he writes, "would be respected as if His Majesty were there in person."

Soldiers have been at work all over the house, tearing everything apart and heaping piles of furnishings in each room, readying the contents for destruction. With the preparations now complete, General Ross dispatches a detail of soldiers to Frenchy Nardin's saloon just opposite the Treasury Building. They're to bring back torches for lighting the fires, he orders.

It's nearly midnight when the men return, armed with long pine poles. Around the poles are wound great wads of blazing cotton. Under the direction of the efficient Lieutenant Pratt, the men go from room to room, setting fire to the piles of furnishings. Charges of powder that have been laid in the basement are beginning to explode. From the first floor the fire ranges along the grand staircase and roars upward until it pours through the roof. Less than fifteen minutes later, the President's House is enveloped by a solid mass of flames.

The British now turn their attention to the brick Treasury Building across the street. One group is sent into the structure to collect whatever paper money they can find. Their search is in vain. Even the fireproof vault in the basement, which they break open, contains only old records. Not one piece of paper money can be found anywhere. No matter, says Ross. Set fire to the building anyway.

Now, General Ross and his officers retire to Mrs. Suter's boarding house for the supper which the commander had ordered earlier this evening. Minutes later, Admiral Cockburn rides his mule through the front door. In high spirits the Admiral struts over to the table and blows out the candles, explaining that he prefers to dine by the light of the fires which are destroying the Americans' capital city.

After the meal is finished, General Ross begins to assemble his troops for return to the camp on Capitol Hill. One officer suggests there's still the War Department building to be burned; Ross vetoes this idea. It can wait until tomorrow. The men are tired and need a night's rest, he adds.

Admiral Cockburn and his detachment follow several blocks behind Ross. When they near McKeowin's Hotel, the Admiral halts the men and strides over to a small group of residents standing beside the hotel. Where is the office of the *Daily National Intelligencer?* Cockburn wants to know. Then as if to explain his question, he adds, "Gales has been telling some tough stories about me." Mail Contractor Bailey, who drives the stage between New York and Washington City, says he's a stranger in town and knows nothing about the newspa-

per. Two other men in the group also plead ignorance concerning the whereabouts of Editor Gales or the location of his office.

Infuriated, the Admiral turns on them, his eyes blazing with anger. They had better loosen their tongues or he'll give them a taste of a British jail. Thus intimidated, the men confess that the office is on the south side of Pennsylvania Avenue at Sixth Street.

Throughout the evening thick black clouds have been hovering overhead. Now the rain begins, a hard, pelting rain that drenches the soldiers. But Cockburn is not to be stopped by anything so inconsequential. He orders his men to follow as he hurries over to the *Daily National Intelligencer* office. A sentry is instructed to stand guard on the street, the usual military precaution whenever a detachment halts. Then Cockburn directs one of his officers to break down the door. The Admiral wants a report on what is inside. A few minutes later the redcoat emerges, saying that the establishment contains only books, cases of type, and a printing press.

"Burn it down," roars Cockburn. But just at this moment two residents of the block, Mrs. Pontius D. Stelle and Mrs. Brush, come forward. They plead with the Admiral not to set fire to the office; if he does that, their homes will be destroyed too.

Cockburn listens patiently. Very well, he'll wreck the office rather than burn it down. But that little task can wait until tomorrow morning. "Never fear, ladies; be tranquil," he says in a patronizing tone. "You are much safer under my administration than you were under Jemmy Madison's." Having uttered this reassurance, Cockburn and his men now move off through the driving rain, following along behind General Ross and his detachment. For the remaining hours before dawn, they'll retire to the encampment on Capitol Hill.

For the few residents still in Washington City, this has been a night of terror. Some have huddled in churches; others have watched the flames surging upward, horror-stricken by the devastation the British have wrought. Hundreds have fled to the homes of friends and relatives outside the District . . . hundreds more have simply been roaming through nearby woods and fields, stunned with fright.

Meanwhile, President Madison and his aides had planned to meet Dolley at Salona, the home of Reverend John Maffitt, three miles above the Little Falls bridge. When the President arrives, his wife is not there. The roads are so clogged with retreating militia that the First Lady and her party realize they will never reach the appointed rendezvous tonight.

Instead, they stop at Rokeby, the home of Mrs. Madison's friend, Mathilda Lee Love. Though the solicitous Mrs. Love does everything to make Dolley comfortable, the First Lady finds that sleep is impossible. She sits silently beside her bedroom window, gazing at the angry fires now slowly being quenched by welcome rain. Where is her husband? What's happened to him? And what does the future hold for the devastated capital?

Back in Washington City the British have ended their activities for the night. But outside the office of the *Daily National Intelligencer* the sentry continues to pace back and forth along Pennsylvania Avenue. Admiral Cockburn had forgotten to relieve him when the troops returned to their encampment. Now, one lone redcoat guards the captured capital of the United States.

Eleven
A CITY IN RUINS

For more than a year Admiral Cockburn has wanted revenge. To invade Washington City and destroy the government of this upstart nation has been his all-consuming desire. Now on the morning after the big burning, the lusty Admiral is up at 5 A.M. to enjoy his day of triumph. He confiscates a small gray horse from a nearby stable to replace the mule he was forced to ride yesterday.

Ordering three redcoats to accompany him, the Admiral gallops down Pennsylvania Avenue to inspect the damage done to the President's House. It's a rewarding sight. Only the smoke-blackened outside walls are still standing. Even the lightning rod on the roof of the house has been twisted and bent by the intense heat. Poking gingerly through the smoldering ruins, Cockburn chuckles with pleasure. Everything has been reduced to ashes . . . there is nothing left of little Jemmy's palace.

Out in Georgetown, Dr. William Thornton has spent a sleepless night. He is frantic with worry about his precious Patent Bureau. The Bureau is located in a three-story brick structure, once known as Blodgett's Hotel, at the northeast corner of Eighth and E Streets, Northwest. Samuel Blodgett had operated a hostelry here for several years. Then in 1810 the government purchased the building to house both the Post Office Department and the Patent Bureau. Here are stored several hundred models that have been submitted for patents, models that represent the inventive genius of the entire nation. Here, too, are a number of Dr. Thornton's own inventions—boilers, firearms, and various musical instruments. The burning of these models would be a disaster far greater than he cares to imagine.

Early this morning Thornton comes to a decision. He'll ask his host, Dr. Peter, for the fastest horse in his stable and set out for Washington City. Someway, somehow, he must persuade the British to leave the Patent Bureau untouched.

By 8 A.M. Admiral Cockburn has returned to the encampment on Capitol Hill where General Ross is organizing his forces to complete the destruction upon which they had embarked last night. The first detachment, commanded by Major Waters, is armed with gunpowder and rockets. Two-by-two, the men file down the muddy Avenue, heading for the Treasury Building. Last night's thundershower put out the flames before they had made much headway. Now, new fires must be started.

Once the Treasury Building is blazing satisfactorily, the troops move on to a structure just west of the President's House. It's the building occupied by the State, War, and Navy Departments. A detail of soldiers is sent inside to ransack the rooms. Records, papers, documents—all are strewn over the floors to make the structure more inflammable, once the rockets have been fired. In less than an hour, the destruction is complete; surging flames have engulfed the building, collapsing the walls and reducing the contents to ashes.

Satisfied with the burning ruins, Major Waters orders his men to proceed west on F Street to the old hotel now used by the Post Office Department and the Patent Bureau. When they arrive, Waters instructs four soldiers to break down the doors with axes.

Just at this moment Dr. William Thornton gallops up and begins remonstrating with Major Waters. The patents granted by the United States are the property of private citizens, not the government. And haven't the British pledged that they will not harm any private property? Further, Thornton questions, "Are you Englishmen or vandals? This is the Patent Office, a depository of the ingenuity of the American nation, in which the whole of the civilized world is interested. Would you destroy it?"

Major Waters looks dubious. Noting the hesitant manner of the officer, Dr. Thornton warns him that "to burn what would be useful to all mankind would be as barbarous as to burn the Alexandria Library, for which the Turks have been condemned by all enlightened nations."

Waters is thoroughly confused. He knows that General Ross does not approve of destroying private property. If the Patent Bureau is filled with models belonging to individuals, and not to the government, he doesn't care to take the responsibility for firing the building. Very well, he finally agrees. Dr. Thornton must consult his commanding officer, Colonel Jones, who is several blocks away. Waters promises to wait until he has further word from the Colonel.

The doctor races off to confront Jones with similar arguments. The models are private property, he insists; nothing in the Patent Bureau belongs to the government. Won't the Colonel countermand his order to burn the building? Jones agrees at least to postpone the destruction and sends a messenger back to Major Waters, reporting his decision. Perhaps later the building can be burned, but not until he has clarified the matter with General Ross.

In the meantime, Admiral Cockburn has arrived at the *Daily National Intelligencer* office with a detail of soldiers. For the past year Cockburn has read occasional issues of the newspaper and has been enraged by what Editor Gales has written about the Admiral. Now he gleefully announces, "I'll punish Madison's man Joe as I have the master, Jemmy." The soldiers are ordered to cart out the several hundred books in the editor's library and burn them on Pennsylvania Avenue. Next, the printing press is shoved through the door to be pounded into scrap iron.

So exhilarated is the Admiral that he forgets his dignity as an officer and assists in carrying out the cases of type, dumping them into the road and trampling the letters into the mud. "Be sure all the C's in the boxes are destroyed," he shouts to his men, "so that the rascals can have no further means of abusing my name."

A small group of onlookers has gathered near the office to watch the enemy soldiers. One bold man among the spectators calls out to Cockburn, "If General Washington had been still alive, Admiral, you would never have got here so easily."

"Sir," retorts the British officer, "if General Washington had been President, we would never have thought to come here."

Around 2 P.M. a detachment of two hundred redcoats and four officers leave the Capitol Hill encampment, heading down Delaware Avenue. Their destination is Greenleaf's Point, the American fort situated on a finger of land jutting out into the Potomac River just southwest of the city. Most of the buildings have already been destroyed by the Yankees, but the British officers have orders to get rid of the powder magazine, the storehouse which contains more than one hundred barrels of gunpowder.

Unknown to the enemy, the Americans have hidden much of the gunpowder in an old dry well near the magazine. Junked guns and other useless artillery have been heaped on top of the powder barrels to conceal the cache. The redcoats now lay trails of powder which lead to the magazine. Torches are readied to set off the powder. Then, quite accidentally, one soldier drops his torch down the dry well.

Within seconds there is an earthshaking explosion. Stones, bricks, guns, chunks of clay and mangled bodies are flung through the air. Roofs of nearby houses are torn off; windows are shattered. To the terrified Englishmen, this is far worse than anything they have experienced at Bladensburg. Twelve men are killed, thirty wounded—some critically. Redcoats, numb from shock, carry the injured back to a hospital which is hastily set up in a deserted house near the Capitol.

Even before the disaster at Greenleaf's Point, General Ross had made up his mind that it was time to get his troops back to the fleet anchored at Benedict. He has already accomplished his purpose in coming to Washington City; the government buildings are in ruins. There have been rumors that General Winder is regrouping his forces out in the countryside . . . that Virginia is calling up thousands of militia . . . that Maryland has thousands more waiting to assault the British soldiers. He's already decided to pull out tonight.

However, before Ross can begin breaking camp, another calamity strikes. All day long the soldiers have been sweltering under a blanket of heat. At 4 P.M. gigantic black clouds begin rolling in from the northwest, punctuated with crashing thunder and wild zigzags of lightning. The sky grows darker and darker until a midnightlike gloom covers the city. The first drops of rain soon become blinding sheets of water. Hurricane winds crumple houses, blow down brick buildings. The air is filled with whirling debris. Great trees are uprooted, tossed about like small toys. The tornado that has struck Washington City is something the British have never before experienced. Paralyzed with fright, the redcoats throw themselves on the ground or huddle against the blackened walls of the Capitol. Soldiers who have defied the Americans' bullets are now terrorized by the violence of Nature in this strange country.

Soon after 6 P.M. the storm begins to subside. General Ross calls his officers together and explains the strategy for tonight's withdrawal. Wagons must be rounded up to carry away the wounded. Campfires are to be built encircling the encampment on Capitol Hill, campfires large enough to be seen for many miles. A few redcoats from each company will be detailed to move around the fires, as if they are preparing the evening meal. Thus, should any Americans be watching, there will be a definite impression that the British are getting ready for a second night of occupation.

When darkness falls, the men begin stealing away by twos and threes, heading back to the turnpike gate at the edge of the city. By 9 P.M. the last soldiers have left the campfires. The British now regroup into companies and begin the march back through Bladensburg. The soldiers who were left there will then form up and the entire force will start out for Benedict where they expect to rejoin the fleet.

During the twenty-five hours the Englishmen have occupied the capital city, millions of dollars worth of damage has been done. They have accomplished far more devastation than they had ever thought possible in such a short time. Ross and Cockburn congratulate each other on having thoroughly humiliated the American people.

Throughout this frantic Thursday, President Madison and the First Lady have spent most of their time driving around the Virginia countryside searching for each other. This morning the President had ridden from Maffitt's home in Salona over to Wren's Tavern at Falls Church, hoping Dolley would be there. Meanwhile, the First Lady had set out for Maffitt's home, only to be told upon her arrival that her husband had already left. Just before the tornado struck, they finally met at Wiley's Tavern on Difficult Run.

It was a joyous reunion. Even the storm raging outside was forgotten. Until the moment when Dolley saw her husband walk through the tavern door, she was certain he had been captured by the British. Now all the pent-up fears vanished. They were together again. To the First Lady that was all that mattered.

By midnight, however, President Madison and his aides decide they must rejoin General Winder over in Maryland. Wait here at Wiley's Tavern, the President tells Dolley. When Washington City is once again safe, he'll send for her. In the meantime Winder needs all the support he can get.

The tearful First Lady waves to her husband as the Presidential party rides off through the rainy night. To have her darling little husband leave now, not knowing when she will see him again, is frightening. Yet she understands the responsibilities that are weighing upon him. The fate of the nation must come first!

Twelve

WILL THEY RETURN?

An eerie silence fills the deserted streets of Washington City on this Friday morning, August 26. Poplar trees, uprooted by yesterday's violent winds, lie at crazy angles, half-blocking the broad expanse of Pennsylvania Avenue. The rubble, the debris created by the tornado, coupled with the burned-out government buildings give the town a ghostlike appearance. Word circulates that the British have left, but few care to venture outside.

Fortunately, there's been no slave rebellion. Wild rumors that the black men would rise up against their masters, that they would join the British in destruction of the city—all have proven false. But now there's a new threat. Looters!

The poor people here have long been a problem. Drifters, unskilled workmen who were hired to help with the public buildings, have stayed on after their jobs were finished. When they had no more money, these men simply lived by their wits, stealing what they could to eke out a bare existence. Now, without soldiers to patrol the streets, with the mayor and government officials out of town, all semblance of authority is gone. The looters are taking over. Running in and out of empty houses and buildings, rummaging through smoking ruins, they help themselves to anything they can find.

Out at Georgetown about 8 A.M. word reaches Dr. Thornton that the enemy has pulled out of Washington City. His first thought is for the Patent Bureau. He *must* know—is the building still standing? The Thorntons make quick work of packing up and hasten back to town. Leaving his wife at their home on F Street, Dr. Thornton drives on to the Patent Bureau. Yes, there it is. The roof has been damaged by the tornado but a walk through the building reassures the doctor that nothing has been touched. His precious models are all in place.

There's another disturbing problem, though. It's evident that much looting is taking place. And that must

be stopped! Because he was once a justice of the peace, Thornton now decides to assume the role of temporary mayor. Guards are enlisted to patrol the ruins of the President's House, the Capitol, the other government buildings. Gradually the looters are driven out; within a few hours order is restored.

When Mayor Blake returns at midafternoon, he is somewhat embarrassed. He had no idea that the town was in such a state of confusion. But he's also indignant that Dr. Thornton has usurped the Mayor's authority. With all this looting going on, someone had to . . . the doctor retorts, furious that the mayor doesn't appreciate what he has done to bring the situation under control.

Last night when President Madison and his aides left Wiley's Tavern, they had planned to cross the Potomac River at Conn's Ferry. On arriving there, they found that the boat was not operating. They had to wait until dawn this morning before they could reach the Maryland shore. It's now nearly 6 P.M. when the weary travelers ride into Montgomery Court House, anxious for a conference with General Winder. They are told word was received earlier in the day that the enemy had withdrawn from Washington City. The General left at noon, accompanied by Secretary of State Monroe and a meager force of regrouped militia. They are heading for Baltimore because Winder believes that's where the next encounter with the British will take place.

Exhausted though he is from a long day in the saddle, President Madison says they must move on . . . try to catch up with Winder. By 9 P.M. the President realizes that going farther tonight is futile. He halts the party at Brookeville, a tiny Quaker community, and inquires if they might spend the night at the home of Caleb and Henrietta Bentley.

Brookeville is usually a quiet village. But during the past few days it has been teeming with displaced soldiers and civilians. Though her religion opposes war, Mrs. Bentley has welcomed all who have knocked at her door, gladly supplying food for the many flocking into town. She has told them all: "It is against our principles to have anything to do with war, but we receive and relieve all who come to us."

In answer to President Madison's request, the Bentleys welcome him and his party as honored guests. Servants are directed to prepare supper immediately; beds are spread out in the parlor; guards are stationed around the house. Madison is pleased to find old friends here, too. The former editor of the *Daily National Intelligencer*, Samuel Harrison Smith, and his wife are also temporarily residing with the Bentleys.

Before long everyone in the village knows about the famous overnight guests. Young and old alike throng into the Bentley house to shake hands with their President. Later this evening Mrs. Smith describes the event in a letter to her sister. Of Madison she writes,

"He was tranquil as usual, and though much distressed by the dreadful event which had taken place, not dispirited."

After the villagers depart, the President asks Mrs. Bentley for a quiet place where he might do some work. The hostess takes him into her husband's study, pointing to the comb-back Windsor chair with a small writing table attached to the arm. Here's a quill pen, she says, and some blotting sand. After lighting several candles around the room, she leaves her guest alone. Because Secretary Monroe is the one man upon whom he can depend for good advice, especially during wartime, Madison writes him: "I will either wait here for you to join me, or follow and join you, as you may think best. . . . If you decide on coming hither, the sooner the better."

Out at Snell's Bridge, where General Winder has set up camp for the night, Secretary Monroe is having second thoughts about accompanying the troops to Baltimore. It now appears that Winder is mistaken about the destination of the enemy. Scouts have just reported the British are heading back to their ships anchored at Benedict. There are also well-confirmed rumors that the abandoned capital is in a state of chaos . . . looters are running wild.

In view of all this, Secretary Monroe decides he must inform the President. His penciled dispatch urges Mr.

Madison to return to Washington City as soon as possible. There's a definite need, Monroe adds, to bring some strong central authority to the riotous confusion that now exists.

Very early on Saturday morning, August 27, a messenger delivers Monroe's dispatch to the Bentley home. After reading it, President Madison again retires to the quiet of his host's study. Notes must be sent to his Cabinet members at once, asking that they come back to the capital as soon as possible.

When these are finished, Madison feels free to write a more pleasurable letter—one to his beloved Dolley:

Brookeville

My Dearest:

Finding that our army has left Montgomery County Court House, we pushed on to this place, with a view to join it, or proceed to the City, as further information may prescribe.

I have just received a line from Col. Monroe saying that the enemy were out of Washington and on the retreat to their ships and advising our immediate return to Washington. We shall accordingly set out thither immediately; you will of course take the same resolution.

I know not where we are in the first instance to hide our heads but shall look for a place upon my arrival. . . .

Truly yours,
J. M.

At midmorning the President is surprised to see Secretary Monroe rein up in the Bentley yard. Monroe confesses that he's come to reinforce the urgency of the message he drafted last night. There's no need for that, says Madison. Arrangements have already been made to return to Washington City. Escorted by a guard of twenty mounted infantrymen, the President and his party ride off at noon, waving cheerful farewells to their host and hostess. Now, with Monroe at his side, James Madison feels a new surge of confidence. Certainly together they can solve the problems awaiting them at the capital.

It's 5 P.M. when the Presidential group arrives in Washington City. James Madison is near collapse. For almost five days he's practically lived on horseback, spending from fifteen to twenty hours each day in the saddle. There are those who have accused him of thinking more of his own safety than that of the capital. But, as President of the United States, Madison has felt that it's his solemn duty not to allow himself to be captured by the invading enemy. He's done his utmost to keep in contact with General Winder and the army, lending the support of his office to boost the morale of the troops. For a sixty-three-year-old man in frail health, the stamina which he has exhibited can only be attributed to his strong devotion to his country.

The President and Secretary Monroe ride directly to

the home of Attorney General Rush, where they spend several hours conferring on the military and political situation. Around 8:30 P.M. the men are startled by the sound of cannon fire which seems to be coming from downriver. Then there's a thunderous explosion. Has Fort Washington been attacked? Is this a new naval assault by the enemy? They listen intently; there's only an ominous silence.

The three men conclude that nothing further can be accomplished tonight and the weary President retires to the home of his brother-in-law, Richard Cutts. Because Cutts now owns the house on F Street which the Madisons rented when they first came to Washington City, there's a familiarity about these surroundings which heartens the President. Yet he's haunted by thoughts of Dolley. Is she still safe at Wiley's Tavern? Will she be in danger on her return trip?

Soon after dawn on Sunday, August 28, Madison orders his horse saddled. Together with Monroe and Rush, he rides out toward Fort Washington. Even before they reach the Fort, ten miles down the Potomac River, there's evidence that the garrison has been blown up.

What has happened? the President inquires. He is told that Captain Sam Dyson, who commanded the fort, had been ordered by General Winder to blow it up if attacked by land forces. He was *not* attacked by land, but cannon fire from the British fleet sailing up the river threw Dyson into a panic. He had ordered the sixty men stationed at the garrison to leave, then set off the great stores of powder in the fort's magazine.

Madison is appalled by the stupidity of such an act. Now enemy ships will have clear sailing northward. It's already rumored that another fleet of British ships has been sighted on the Potomac River, that Alexandria is the next town to be attacked. If that invasion should be successful, what's to prevent the British from coming on up to Washington City? Preparations must be made at once to protect the capital. The President asks Secretary Monroe to take charge of setting up defensive measures.

Still worried about the First Lady, Madison returns to the Cuttses' home and writes to warn her of this new development:

My Dearest:

I cannot yet learn what has been the result. Should the port have been taken, the British ships with their barges will be able to throw the city again into alarm, and you may be again compelled to retire from it, which I find would have a disagreeable effect. Should the ships have failed in their attack, you cannot return too soon. . . . In the meantime, it will be best for you to remain in your present quarters. . . .

Ever and most aff'y yours,
J. M.

By noon the President learns that the citizens of Alexandria have agreed to surrender all ships and cargo awaiting export if the enemy promises not to bombard their homes and shops. Before long, all Washington City knows of Alexandria's action. Panic spreads. Will their city be next? people ask each other.

Now the President decides to inspect the ruins of the Capitol building. Perhaps his very presence, riding through the streets, will give the citizens some much-needed confidence. Even before he is in the saddle, Dr. Thornton comes running over from next door. "The people are violently irritated at the thought of our attempting to make any more futile resistance," Thornton tells the President. Furthermore, a group is planning to approach British Captain Gordon and ask for surrender terms.

Madison explodes with fury. "Never! Never!" he shouts. Anyone who attempts to make such an idiotic move "will be repelled by the bayonet."

At midafternoon the First Lady returns to Washington City. As her carriage passes the President's House, she is shocked at the sight of her former home. Everything is gone. Only a shell remains—the walls blackened by smoke, the interior a mass of ashes, the ground littered with debris. She turns her head away as tears run down her cheeks.

Driving on to the Cuttses' home, Dolley is welcomed

by her sister. The President, she is told, is still out inspecting the city . . . he should return soon. The First Lady wants to freshen her appearance. Four days of wandering have left her bedraggled.

Within the hour President Madison reins up outside. Dolley is waiting in the Cuttses' doorway and embraces James when he enters the house. What a happy surprise, her husband says, to have his dearest wife back again. But there may be more danger ahead. Didn't she receive his second note? Dolley shakes her head, explaining that she left as soon as his letter from Brookeville arrived. It makes no difference . . . all that matters now is that they are together again.

Before long Secretary Monroe is at the door, asking for some time with the President. He wants to report on the defensive measures he's taken to protect the capital. A fort will be erected on Windmill Hill near the southeast waterfront. The District of Columbia militia, commanded by General Smith, has been called out to man the defense.

While the two men are conferring, Dolley picks up yesterday's issue of the Richmond *Enquirer* which has been left on the parlor table. Opening the newspaper, she turns to the editorial page. What she sees is too good to keep to herself. The First Lady interrupts the conference, asking her husband to read aloud the paragraphs she indicates. He begins:

For the benefit of our citizens let it also be recollected that when Philadelphia, then the seat of our government, then a large and populous town, was taken by the enemy during the war of the Revolution, it struck no terror into the American soil. No man looked down. No man cowered. The war ended gloriously; for it procured us the greatest boon which could be worn by a brave people.

Who then desponds? The power of the State is in motion. The man who is at the head of it is an energetic officer—who deserves and possesses our confidence.

A slow smile spreads across James Madison's face as his eyes meet Dolley's.

Thirteen

IN THE WEEKS
THAT FOLLOW

Late on the night of August 28 Samuel Harrison Smith
and his wife, Margaret, returned from the Bentley home
in Brookeville. On this Monday morning, August 29,
Margaret writes her sister describing the desolate scene
which greeted them as they entered the capital:

We looked at the public buildings, but none were so

thoroughly destroyed as the House of Representatives and the President's House. Those beautiful pillars in the Representatives Hall were crack'd and broken; the roof, that noble dome, painted and carved with such beauty and skill, lay in ashes in the cellars beneath the smoldering ruins, were yet smoking.

In the President's House not an inch, but its crack'd and blacken'd walls remain'd. That scene, when I last visited it, was so splendid throng'd with the great, the gay, the ambitious placemen, and patriotic Heroes was now nothing but ashes, and was it these ashes, now trodden under foot by the rabble, which once possess'd the power to inflate pride, to gratify vanity?

Who would have thought that this mass, so solid, so magnificent, so grand, which seem'd built for generations to come, should by the hands of a few men and in the space of a few hours, be thus irreparably destroy'd?

Mrs. Smith closes her letter in a despondent mood. "It is not to be expected," she concludes, "that Washington City will ever again be the seat of Government."

Others, too, are very depressed when it becomes known that British Captain Gordon has begun seizing the loaded cargo ships at the port of Alexandria which the citizens surrendered in return for a British promise that the town will not be touched. Why—Alexandria is only six miles downstream. Will the enemy next attempt a second invasion of the capital?

Over at the Cuttses' residence on F Street, President Madison receives word from officials in New York City. Now that the capital is in ruins, they presume the government will be moved to another location and they offer a choice of several handsome buildings. Philadelphia authorities have the same idea. Won't Congress return to its former quarters on Chestnut Street?

The President realizes there is no time to lose, if Washington City is to remain the capital. He convenes his Cabinet at noon today. After reassuring the members that defensive measures have been taken to guard the city against further invasion, Madison says that he is calling a special session of Congress for September 19.

Since the old Blodgett Hotel—the structure which houses the Post Office Department and the Patent Bureau—is the only government building still standing, the President proposes that it be used as a meeting place for Congress. The men nod agreement. Secretary Monroe is directed to inform Dr. Thornton that he must find another place for storage of his models. Arrangements will be made at once to convert the building into a temporary home for the lawmakers. Madison merely mentions the offers from New York and Philadelphia, but adds, "Of course we shall carry on here on the banks of the Potomac, where the will of the people has placed the capital."

Late this afternoon Secretary of War Armstrong shows up and is shocked to learn that local citizens are furious with him. They are blaming the Secretary for the present disaster. Stories are circulating that he deliberately plotted the destruction of the city so that the capital would be moved north.

President Madison is well aware of the wave of indignation sweeping the town. There are some who blame the administration, but most people are concentrating their resentment more specifically on the Secretary of War. Tonight Madison rides over to Armstrong's lodging for a talk. In self-defense, the Secretary insists that the anger exhibited by the people has been inspired by intrigue, that all charges are false. He's done everything he was told to do.

The President points out that Armstrong's primary job was not only to follow orders, but to devise plans on his own initiative, especially plans for the defense of the capital. This he failed to do. Perhaps it would be best if the Secretary leave town immediately before any violence occurs. Armstrong agrees and promises to send his resignation tomorrow morning.

During the next few days President Madison spends much of his time on horseback, riding through the streets to calm frightened citizens. Windmill Point is well fortified, he tells them. Adequate troops have been called up. There's no reason to panic.

At 5 A.M. on September 2 British Captain Gordon leaves Alexandria, leading his squadron of ships downstream, including twenty-one captured vessels loaded

with tobacco, cotton, flour, beef, and sugar. When the news reaches Washington City that Captain Gordon is heading south, there is much rejoicing. All fears of a second invasion of the capital are at last dispelled. Now the business of rebuilding can begin.

Over at the office of the *Daily National Intelligencer* the presses are once again humming. Editor Gales has managed to borrow enough equipment from various Baltimore printers to resume publication of his newspaper. In answer to rumors that the seat of government is to be moved to another location, Gales editorializes:

We say boldly that such a measure would be a treacherous breach of faith of the nation, pledged by a solemn law enacted under a constitutional provision. . . . It would be kissing the rod the enemy has wielded; it would be deserting the seat of government at the dictation of an enemy.

By the time Congress assembles on September 19, President Madison has arranged temporary quarters for the various departments of government. The War office has been set up in a building adjoining the Bank of the Metropolis. The State Department operates out of a private home. The Treasury is situated in the former British Minister's residence. The Navy Department is located in a house near the West Market. Now the documents and valuables can be brought back from various hiding places out in the country.

Although public opinion favors the idea of keeping the capital in Washington City, some of the Senators and

Representatives voice loud complaints. "Here we are in the Patent Office," objects Representative Stockton of New Jersey, "in a room not large enough to furnish a seat for each member when all are present, although every spot, up to the fireplace and windows, is occupied." There's talk about moving to another location—possibly New York City.

A group of local landowners becomes alarmed. This must not happen; they have too much money invested in real estate ventures here. Spearheaded by Thomas Law, the group solicits private subscriptions to build a new home for Congress. Law secures promises from carpenters and bricklayers that within four months the structure will be finished, a building that will be known as the "Little Capitol." When Law presents this proposal to the Congressmen, there's no further thought of abandoning Washington City.

One of the most severe losses in the burning of the Capitol was the destruction of the seven hundred forty books which constituted the Congressional Library. Soon after the Senators and Representatives open their special session, a letter from former President Thomas Jefferson arrives. Now in retirement at Monticello, Jefferson wishes to present the nation with his complete library—a collection of books which he has chosen over the past forty years.

A grateful Congress accepts the offer and votes to reimburse the former President with a check for

$23,900. Before many days elapse, a long wagon train sets out from Monticello, winding down the Virginia mountain side. The driver will receive five dollars a day for transporting the books to Washington City. These fine volumes will more than compensate for those lost in the Capitol fire.

Meanwhile, President Madison has contacted Architects Benjamin Latrobe and James Hoban. Latrobe has agreed to supervise the rebuilding of the Capitol. Hoban will return with his original designs for the President's House and try to reconstruct the executive mansion in precise detail. Editor Gales is favorably impressed with the President's persistence. He comments in the *Daily National Intelligencer:* "The British have burned and pillaged but posterity is assured of enjoying a determined nation's restoration to these shrines."

Ever since their return to Washington City, the Madisons have been staying at the Cuttses' home on F Street. Mrs. Cutts is delighted to have her sister; they've always enjoyed each other's company. James is rarely there during the day. He spends most of his time on horseback; the saddle has become his temporary office.

The Thorntons are also pleased to have their old friends so close. However, one aspect of the Madisons' prolonged visit next door troubles Dr. Thornton. The President of the United States holds the highest office in the nation. Shouldn't the dignity of this office require that a suitable home be found for the Chief Executive?

Taking matters into his own hands, Thornton calls on Colonel Benjamin Tayloe, now residing at O'Neill's Hotel. After exchanging pleasantries, the doctor comes straight to the point. Would Tayloe consider leasing Octagon House to the government? It would make a fine residence for the President and First Lady while their former home is being restored.

Tayloe asks time to consider the matter. He has disliked many of the decisions James Madison has made during his administration. But perhaps political differences should be forgotten in the present crisis. The house *is* vacant; French Minister Serurier moved to Philadelphia several weeks ago. A few days later Tayloe signs the lease.

By mid-October the Madisons are settled in Octagon House. With their former home in ashes, this is the most impressive residence in the capital. Dolley is delighted. The light, high-ceilinged rooms, the many fireplaces, and the handsome furniture give the house an air of gracious elegance.

On one side of the marble-floored circular entry hall is the great drawing room; on the other, the dining room where the portrait of George Washington, recently returned, now hangs. Back of the hall is a small reception area. Here the oval staircase curves gently upward in one continual flow to the third floor.

The First Lady is puzzled by the tiny ivory button set in the mahogany handrail at the foot of the stairway. It's

called a "peace point," Dr. Thornton explains. This is traditional in the houses he designs. The button indicates that construction was completed in a satisfactory manner and the owner has paid for the house.

Kitchen quarters in the basement are solidly bricked; a large fireplace and huge ovens provide ample space for cooking. The servants' stairway leading to the dining room insures efficient service as well as private access to the bedrooms on the upper floors. With French John, Sukey, Jim Smith, Paul Jennings, and John Freeman now returned to staff the household, Dolley feels free to resume her entertaining. She's already planning a series of receptions.

The First Lady insists that her husband use the circular room above the entry hall as his study. From its three huge windows the President will have a splendid view of the boats sailing up and down the Potomac River. The windows are framed by yellow draperies, an effective contrast to the dark green walls. In the center of the room is a round table covered with gold-stamped green leather. Around its circumference are wedge-shaped drawers for filing.

After dark, when the candles in the brass wall sconces and the center chandelier are lighted, the study has a cheerful atmosphere. But for more intensive work, the President prefers the brass candlestick on his table. An adjustable spring permits the candle to be raised in the holder as it burns down, insuring continual light.

During the fall, British newspapers begin arriving in the capital. People are amazed to learn that many Englishmen have been horrified by the burning of Washington City. The editor of the London *Statesman* writes:

Willingly would we throw a veil of oblivion over our transactions at Washington. The Cossacks spared Paris, we spared not the capital of America.

The Liverpool *Mercury* sounds an ominous warning, proclaiming that "the fires in Washington would ignite the American soul." And furthermore, the editorial continues:

We will content ourselves by asking the most earnest friends of the conflagratory system, what purpose will be served by the flames of the Senate House at Washington? If the people of the United States retain any portion of that spirit with which they successfully contended for their independence, the effect of these flames will not easily be extinguished.

The capital is now humming with activity. Once the rubble has been cleared away, rebuilding of the devastated areas begins. Day after day, slow-moving carts creak into town, carrying loads of bricks, limestone, and much-needed construction materials. President Madison enjoys riding through the streets to watch the activity. He's cheered by the sight of the laborers, often singing as they work. There's so much to be done, yet there's no lack of enthusiasm among the local citizens.

As the weeks pass, it begins to appear as if the momentum of the enemy drive may be sputtering to a close. After leaving the capital on August 25, the British centered their efforts on Baltimore. Meanwhile, a young Washington City lawyer, Francis Scott Key, had become very concerned about the prominent physician, Dr. William Beanes, who had been taken prisoner by the British. After obtaining permission from President Madison, Key approached Admiral Cockburn and General Ross, asking for the doctor's release. The British officers finally agreed, but detained both Key and Beanes because of their plans for attack. The two men spent the night on the ship's deck, watching the bombardment of Fort McHenry. As the first streaks of dawn appeared, Key saw that the American flag was still flying; the redcoats had failed to capture the fort. Overjoyed, the young lawyer pulled out an old envelope from his pocket and began jotting down verses for a song he called "The Star-Spangled Banner."

By late September news has arrived that the Americans have been victorious in a fierce battle at Plattsburg, New York. Still, there's the haunting fear that Captain Gordon may be taking his squadron of British ships down to New Orleans. Is that quaint little town, so recently acquired by former President Jefferson, in imminent danger of being captured?

Night after night President Madison sits alone in his study at Octagon House reviewing the war reports.

Where will Congress find money to continue the fighting? Has another deadlock developed in the peace negotiations?

The President shakes his head sadly. Will this senseless war never end?

Fourteen

"PEACE! PEACE!"

Into New York harbor on February 11, 1815, sails the British sloop-of-war, *Favorite*, a flag of truce flying from her mast. Aboard is Henry Carroll, one of the American secretaries at the peace conference in Ghent, Belgium. The Atlantic crossing has taken thirty-eight days and during that time young Carroll's nail-studded black leather dispatch box has never been out of his sight. Its contents are precious.

It has been almost eight months since the peace commissioners from Great Britain and the United States began their conference at Ghent. Negotiations became deadlocked almost at once. The Americans wanted the treaty to deal with impressment of sailors and the rights of neutral nations. The English insisted on control of the Great Lakes and the dismantling of American forts on the Canadian border.

The talks continued. By mid-October the British had yielded far enough to propose that each country retain the territory which it controlled when the war ended. The Americans had given up the impressment issue but wanted to return to conditions as they existed before the war began.

Early in November the British Parliament received news of one defeat after another in America. Englishmen were sick of both war and high taxes. Parliament was faced with a crucial decision. Should they instruct their commissioners to agree on peace or spend millions of pounds to send more troops to the United States?

Britain's most outstanding general, the Duke of Wellington, was summoned. Would he take command of the war? The Duke's reply startled the politicians. He did not believe that anyone could achieve complete victory in America. His opinion was the decisive factor: Parliament instructed their commissioners to ask the Americans for a draft of their terms.

Finally, on December 24, 1814, the Treaty of Ghent was signed. Though it was not a triumph for either side, the settlement ended a conflict that had been most unpopular in both countries. The London *Times* editorialized: "The war, to speak tenderly of it, has not been a very glorious one. . . . We have attempted to force our principles on the Americans and have failed."

Now, on this Saturday evening, the British *Favorite* anchors in New York harbor. Landing at the Battery, Henry Carroll steps ashore and goes directly to the City Hotel on Broadway for the night. As he signs the register, the young man remarks casually that his black dispatch box contains the peace treaty which he is delivering to President Madison. The news travels quickly. Within half an hour the streets are thronged with men and women carrying lighted candles. Shouts of "Peace! Peace!" echo throughout the city.

Early Sunday morning Carroll hires a post-chaise for the drive to Washington City. He specifies four horses, rather than the usual two; this trip must be made as quickly as possible, he explains to the livery owner. By noon the messenger is on his way, threading through narrow streets still crowded with victory celebrants. After leaving the outskirts of New York City, he turns south toward Philadelphia, then on to Baltimore and the

capital. The ride proves to be a long and tedious one, over rough roads filled with potholes and muddied by a week of rain.

It's nearly dusk on Tuesday afternoon, February 14, when the two-wheeled carriage rattles down Pennsylvania Avenue. Turning into I Street, Carroll stops at the home of Secretary of State Monroe. Rumors of peace have already reached Washington City. Quickly a crowd surrounds the chaise; the messenger, clutching his dispatch box, is cheered as he dashes up the steps to the Secretary's front door. Within a few minutes the two men emerge smiling and drive off down Eighteenth Street to see President Madison.

In his second-floor study at Octagon House the President is poring over a stack of official papers. Occasionally he looks up, staring off into space, his expression grim. Though remarkable progress has been made in rebuilding the capital these past few months, the nation is still involved in a war which no one understands.

Downstairs the great drawing room is filled with Dolley's friends. The First Lady is holding an informal reception to honor her young cousin, Sally Coles, who has just arrived for a visit. There's much talk about Andrew Jackson's recent victory at New Orleans. On the morning of January 8 the British stormed the American defense works in the little Louisiana town. So effectively was the enemy repulsed by General Jackson's forces, that the battle lasted only half an hour; the British quickly withdrew to their ships and departed. And now there are ever-increasing peace reports. Can these rumors possibly be true? everyone asks.

Conversation is interrupted by a loud rap at the front door. French John ushers Secretary Monroe and Henry Carroll into the entry hall. While Monroe warms himself at the iron stove, the messenger throws off his mud-spattered cloak and rushes through the drawing room doorway. He bows low before the First Lady, then whispers something to her. The color rises in Dolley's cheeks; her eyes light up with excitement. She motions toward the circular study above and asks French John to escort the men upstairs.

The dramatic entrance of Henry Carroll causes much speculation among the guests, but Dolley refuses to comment. Whatever announcement is made, she decides, must come from the President.

When Secretary Monroe and Henry Carroll enter the study, Madison greets them warmly. He knows from James Monroe's smile that there is good news. Handing the leather dispatch box to the Chief Executive, Carroll explains that it contains the peace treaty signed at Ghent. The terms must be carefully considered, says the President, adding that he will summon his Cabinet members immediately.

By early evening Octagon House is ablaze with candlelight. People begin streaming through the front door. No one knows yet what the terms of the treaty are. No matter. It's assumed that everything is all right, that the war is over at last. Diplomats, friends, Congressmen from both parties crowd into the drawing room. Tonight all political differences are forgotten.

In the upstairs study the President and members of his Cabinet work quietly. Word by word, they analyze the issues set forth in the treaty. The men cannot allow their

hopes for peace to soar too high until the final paragraph is perused.

Soon after 8 P.M. James Madison makes his way down the curving staircase and enters the drawing room. A hush falls over the guests; everyone waits for the Chief Executive to speak. Smiling broadly, the President announces that the terms are satisfactory. Dolley flings out her arms, crying "Peace! Peace!"

The news electrifies the crowd. Suddenly everyone is shouting, laughing, cheering. Sally Coles runs to the basement stairway and calls to the servants below, repeating Dolley's words. Young Paul Jennings, the black serving boy, grabs his violin and rasps out "The President's March." John Freeman, the butler, is instructed to bring up the wine bottles. Serve everyone liberally, guests and servants alike, adds the First Lady.

The shouts from Octagon House spread rapidly throughout the capital. PEACE! PEACE! Church bells ring; cannons boom; bonfires illuminate the streets. Washington City goes wild with joy.

Three days later, on February 17, the United States Senate ratifies the treaty by unanimous vote. All dissension, all friction among the states vanishes. Peace, with honor, has been achieved. James Madison's hopes, his dreams for this new nation are now renewed.

BIBLIOGRAPHY

Adams, Henry. *History of the United States of America: 1783 through 1865.* 4 volumes. New York: Doubleday, Page and Company, 1909.

Aikman, Lionelle. *The Living White House.* Washington, D.C.: National Geographic Society, 1966.

————. *We, The People: The Story of the United States Capitol.* Washington, D.C.: The United States Capitol Historical Society, 1963.

Ames, Mary Clemmer. *Ten Years in Washington: Life and Scenes in the National Capitol.* Hartford, Conn.: A. D. Worthington and Company, Publishers, 1880.

Ammon, Harry. *James Monroe.* New York: McGraw-Hill Book Company, 1971.

Anthony, Katharine. *Dolly Madison: Her Life and Times.* Garden City, New York: Doubleday and Company, Inc., 1949.

Barney, Mary Chase. *Biographical Memoir of the Late Joshua Barney.* Boston: Gray and Bowen, 1832.

Beirne, Francis F. *The War of 1812.* New York: E. P. Dutton & Company, Inc., 1949.

Brant, Irving. *James Madison: Commander-in-Chief, 1812–1836.* Indianapolis: Bobbs-Merrill Company, 1961.

Bryan, Wilhelmus Bogart. *A History of the National Capital from its Foundation Through the Period of the Adoption of the Organic Act.* 2 volumes. New York: The Macmillan Company, 1914–1916.

Cassell, Frank. *Merchant Congressman in the Young Republic: Samuel Smith of Maryland.* Madison, Wisconsin: University of Wisconsin Press, 1971.

Coles, Harry L. *The War of 1812.* Chicago: University of Chicago Press, 1965.

Cutts, Lucia Bradley. *Memoirs and Letters of Dolly Madison.* Edited by her grandniece. Boston: Houghton, Mifflin Company, 1886.

Dean, Elizabeth Lippincott. *Dolly Madison: The Nation's Hostess.* New York: Lothrop, Lee and Shepard Company, 1928.

Furman, Bess. *White House Profile.* Indianapolis: Bobbs-Merrill Company, Inc., 1951.

Gleig, G. R. *A Narrative of the Campaigns of the British Army at Washington and New Orleans.* London: J. Murray, 1847.

————. *A Subaltern in America.* Edinburgh and London: W. Blackwood and Sons, 1825.

Green, Constance McLaughlin. *Washington: Village and Capital, 1800–1878.* Princeton, New Jersey: Princeton University Press, 1962.

Herron, Paul. *The Story of Capitol Hill.* New York: Coward-McCann, Inc., 1963.

Horsman, Reginald. *The War of 1812.* New York: Alfred A. Knopf, 1969.

Hurd, Charles. *The White House: A Biography.* New York: Harper and Brothers, Publishers, 1940.

Ingersoll, Charles J. *Historical Sketch of the Second War Between the United States of America and Great Britain.* Volume 2. Philadelphia: Lea and Blanchard, 1845–1849.

Ingraham, Edward Duncan. *A Sketch of the Events Which*

Preceeded the Capture of Washington by the British in 1814. Philadelphia: Carey and Hart, 1849.

Jacobsen, Hugh Newell, editor. *A Guide to the Architecture of Washington, D.C.* New York: Frederick A. Praeger, Publishers, 1965.

Jeffries, Ona Griffin. *In and Out of the White House.* New York: Wilfred Funk, Inc., 1960.

Jennings, Paul. *A Colored Man's Reminiscences of James Madison.* Brooklyn, New York: G. C. Beadle, 1865.

Jensen, Amy LaFollette. *The White House and Its Thirty-Three Families.* New York: McGraw-Hill Book Company, Inc., 1962.

Lord, Walter. *The Dawn's Early Light.* New York: W. W. Norton and Company, 1972.

Lossing, Benson J. *The Pictorial Field-Book of the War of 1812.* New York: Harper and Brothers, 1868.

Means, Marianne. *The Woman in the White House.* New York: Random House, 1963.

Mount, Charles Merrill. *Gilbert Stuart.* New York: W. W. Norton and Company, 1964.

"Mrs. Thornton's Diary." Records of the Columbia Historical Society, Volume 19, pp. 172–182.

Mott, Frank Luther. *American Journalism: A History, 1690–1960.* New York: The Macmillan Company, 1962.

Muller, Charles G. *The Darkest Day: 1814.* Philadelphia: J. B. lippincott Company, 1963.

Nell, William C. *Services of Colored Americans in the Wars of 1776 and 1812.* Boston: Robert F. Wallcut, 1852.

Pearce, Mrs. John N. *The White House: An Historic Guide.* Washington, D.C.: The White House Historical Association, 1964.

Shelton, Isabelle. *The White House Today and Yesterday.* New York: Fawcett Publications, 1962.

Smith, Margaret Bayard. *Forty Years of Washington Society.* Edited by Gaillard Hunt. London: T. Fisher Unwin, 1906.

Swanson, Neil H. *The Perilous Fight.* New York: Farrar and Rinehart, 1945.

Tebbel, John. *The Compact History of the American Newspaper.* New York: Hawthorn Books, Inc., 1963.

Tucker, Glenn. *Poltroons and Patriots.* Volume 2. Indianapolis: Bobbs-Merrill Company, Inc., 1954.

Wharton, Anne Hollingsworth. *Social Life in the Early Republic.* Philadelphia: J. B. Lippincott, 1902.

Williams, John S. *History of the Invasion and Capture of Washington.* New York: Harper and Brothers, Publishers, 1857.

Wiltse, Charles M. *The New Nation: 1800–1845.* New York: Hill and Wang, 1961.

Manuscript Division, Library of Congress
   Dolley Madison Papers
   James Madison Papers
   General William Winder Papers
   William Thornton Papers

Newspapers for 1814
   Daily National Intelligencer
   Liverpool Mercury
   London Statesman
   London Times
   New York Post
   Richmond Enquirer

INDEX

INDEX 179

Thornton, Dr. William, 22, 28,
34–38, 150, 155–156, 158
concern for Patent Bureau, 124–
125, 126–127, 134, 135
leaving of Washington City by,
99
Times, London, 164
Tingey, Capt. Thomas, 97, 102,
104
Todd, John, 16
Treasury Department, 153
burning of, 117–118, 125
Treaty of Ghent, 164
troops, American (*see also* militia):
appearance of, 79
move to Washington City, 84
truce, declaration of, 162

United States Congress (*see also*
House of Representatives;
United States Senate):
declaration of war, 7
newspaper reporting on, 30, 32
passage of Embargo Act, 5
temporary home for, 150
United States Senate:
Joint Session of, 23
ratification of peace treaty, 170
votes on declaration of war, 7
Upper Marlboro, Md., 76
invasion of, 74, 77, 79

Van Ness, Major Gen. John P., 43,
45

war, with Great Britain,
declaration of, 7
War Department, burning of, 125

"War Hawks," 7
Washington City (*see also* Federal
City):
burning of, British response to,
159
establishment of, 20
evacuation of, 71–72, 97, 99
invasion of, *see* invasion of Washington City
panic in, 68–75
protection of, 146
rebuilding of, 159
Washington, Pres. George, 19,
20–21, 129
Washington, Martha, 24, 83
Waters, Major, 125, 126
weapons, *see* ammunition
Wellington, Duke of, 163–164
White House, *see* President's House
Winder, Gov. Levin, 11
Winder, Brig. Gen. William Henry,
11, 12, 39–40, 42, 43, 45,
50, 56, 62, 63, 64, 67, 73,
74, 77, 78, 79, 83, 89, 112,
130, 132, 136, 137, 138, 141,
142
assistance to, 87–88
orders of bridge destruction, 85,
86
pull back to Washington City,
84–85
reassurance of citizens by, 70–71
retreat, 94
"victory plan," 81
Wood Yard, 66, 67
American encampment in, 62–
63, 64

ABOUT THE AUTHOR

Mary Kay Phelan's career as a writer began in response to questions from her two young sons. When, after a trip to Washington, she could not find a book that satisfied their demands for more information about the White House, she wrote one herself. And she has continued to write books that bring American history vividly to life. Mrs. Phelan is the author of *Four Days in Philadelphia— 1776,* which tells the story of the adoption of the Declaration of Independence; *Midnight Alarm: The Story of Paul Revere's Ride; The Story of the Great Chicago Fire, 1871; Mr. Lincoln's Inaugural Journey; The Story of the Boston Tea Party; Probing the Unknown: The Story of Dr. Florence Sabin; Martha Berry;* and three books in the Crowell Holiday series—*Mother's Day, The Fourth of July,* and *Election Day.*

Born in Kansas, Mrs. Phelan was graduated from DePauw University in Indiana and received her master's degree in English from Northwestern University. She has worked as an advertising copy writer and she and her husband are now involved in the production of historical films that are widely used in schools and libraries. The Phelans live in Davenport, Iowa, most of the year but enjoy their frequent travels in this country and in Europe.

ABOUT THE ILLUSTRATOR

John Gretzer was born in Council Bluffs, Iowa, attended the University of Omaha, and spent one year at the Kansas City Art Institute, studying under Thomas Hart Benton.

Mr. Gretzer has been active in the production of animated movies and in department-store advertising. He was at one time art director for a publishing firm and now undertakes free-lance assignments involving advertising and editorial art. He is the illustrator of several books for children.

Mr. Gretzer and his family live in Perkasie, Pennsylvania.